Lord, I'm Back Again

YOUNG READERS

LORD, I'M BACK AGAIN

Story Devotions for Girls

MARY PHRANER WARREN

AUGSBURG Publishing House • Minneapolis

LORD, I'M BACK AGAIN

Copyright © 1981 Augsburg Publishing House

Library of Congress Catalog Card No. 81-65651

International Standard Book No. 0-8066-1887-6

All rights reserved. Except for brief quotations in critical articles or reviews, no part of this book may be reproduced in any manner without prior written permission from the publisher. Write to: Permissions, Augsburg Publishing House, 426 S. Fifth St., Box 1209, Minneapolis, MN 55440.

Scripture quotations unless otherwise noted are from the Revised Standard Version of the Bible, copyright 1946, 1952, and 1971 by the Division of Christian Education of the National Council of Churches.

Scripture quotations marked TEV are from the Good News Bible, Today's English Version: Copyright © American Bible Society 1966, 1971, 1976. Used by permission.

Illustrations by Judy Swanson.

MANUFACTURED IN THE UNITED STATES OF AMERICA

*To all the children of the world
who are not afraid
to keep on asking honest questions*

Contents

page	9	About This Book
	11	The Wings of the Morning
	17	Lord, I'm Back Again
	22	It Looks Backwards, But Try It Anyway
	30	I Feel So Different
	36	The Unanswered Question
	45	Mixed Messages
	53	Surprise! Surprise!
	62	This Present Can't Be Wrapped
	69	Candy Finds a Way
	77	The Gift of a Week
	87	Hurrah for Grandma!
	95	There's Room for Three of Us
	102	The Day of Two Floods

About This Book

During these years when you are growing up, you probably have lots of questions. Sometimes these questions don't seem to have any clear answers. Just when you think you've solved a problem after a heated discussion in Sunday school or around the dining-room table, then a situation turns up which makes the opposite seem true.

It is comforting to know you can share these mixed-up times with God. You can tell him your problems in plain, everyday words and be certain he will pay attention to you.

God doesn't always come up with easy answers, mainly because he never did promise us the world would be an easy place to live. But the boys and girls I've talked to have discovered that when they keep on praying, God shows them the right thing to do and say.

No matter how hard they try, grown-ups don't always have time to listen. Luckily God does have time. He loves you all the more when you come to him with questions again and again. So, like the boys and girls in these stories, be sure to talk to him often when you are confused or lonely or hurt. Remember to share with him the times you feel like bursting with happiness too. You will find he is a good friend who will never let you down.

The characters in the following stories are based on real-life children I have known. Part of the fun of being an author is that one is able to take true incidents, change them slightly, and weave them into stories. I have always known I wanted to be an author. In fact, Sandra, the girl who has the Thinking Tree in the story called *I Feel So Different*, is actually me!

I wish to thank Ingeborg MacHaffie and Annette Ross for their suggestions during the time I was writing these stories and our daughter Linda for helping to select the title.

The Wings of the Morning

It happened again. I felt God's nearness. I was on the beach playing alone. I knew, after a while, my folks would be wondering where I was.

I would have felt silly saying "I was just having a little time alone with God." They might have laughed. Does anyone else feel like this? I'd like to share it but I don't know how.

On this golden late summer morning, the Kriegers wouldn't be making the fire for a wiener roast for an hour or so. Dad and Mom had stretched out on the sand to talk a while.

Ginny glanced at her older sister. Flo and her friend Rich were tossing a large blue and white Frisbee to each other.

"Here, Ginny! Catch!" called Rich.

With a wild leap, Ginny grabbed the plastic disk and twirled it toward her sister.

"You two want to take a walk?"

"No, thanks," called Flo. "Maybe later."

"I think Damon will go with you," said Mother. "He's down there near the water's edge building a sand castle. A few minutes ago he was looking for someone to hunt for starfish on the breakwater with him."

"I'll come," agreed Damon as soon as Ginny asked.

He looked as if he had rolled over in the wet sand, so she said patiently, "Well then, sandman, rinse yourself off and let's go."

The tide, on its way out, had sucked at the sand leaving a narrow fringe of foam, stranded crabs, and seashells. The sand flats were appearing.

Ginny and Damon raced on the hard, damp sand along the edge of the ocean, playing tag, splashing through the tide pools. Once they paused to try to catch a minnow.

Most of the pools were only ankle deep, but unexpectedly Damon sank into the soft, sandy bottom of a pool that covered his sturdy legs to the knees. Chuckling, he sat down in it to cool off and emerged dripping.

Ginny laughed. "That one over there is shallow. I bet if we use a clam shell as a scoop, we'll get a minnow after all."

"I'm going to catch a seagull instead," declared her brother. He rubbed his sunburnt nose. "I mean it, Gin. I've wanted one for ages."

Ginny leaned down and gave his wet body a squeeze. "Tell you what. I'll treat you to a cherry pop if you manage to *touch* one of those gulls. See, Damon, the two birds on the big flat are clamming. If they get a clam, they'll carry it high into the air and drop it—kerplunk—onto the rocky breakwater to break the shell. I've seen other gulls do it."

With a new burst of energy, Damon sprinted off, leaving small, firm footprints in the damp sand. Alongside them Ginny recognized the feathery prints of sandpipers and the unmistakable tracks of the gulls. She let him get a good head start, and then overtook him, racing all the way to the breakwater. He'd know immediately if she held back to let him win, so she loped on, far ahead of him now.

"That's because you're in practice from running track," he gasped when he reached the rock where she had perched. "Ginny, can we walk out to the tippy end of the rocks?"

"Sure. Ready?"

For a long time they clambered over the breakwater, hunting for starfish.

"Sometimes we've found four or five," complained Damon down on the sand again with empty hands.

"Here's a sand dollar anyway," offered Ginny. "It's a whole one; that's something."

"My legs are tired," he told her. "I want to go back."

"Go ahead," she said. "Walk up near the tide line, Damon. I'll be along soon."

She watched her brother head toward the distant figures of the family. After a summer at the cove, Damon knew by heart the list of beach safety rules Mom and Dad had pinned on the cottage wall.

Once again Ginny climbed the rocky promontory

and squinted at the ocean sparkling in the sun. Wave after wave crashed in, frothing high into the air.

It looked like the suds when someone poured too much soap into the washing machine. Ginny could never get enough of the ocean. It had pounded inside of her throughout the summer, singing its rhythmic, never-ending tune. Whenever she looked at it, she felt as small as a grain of sand.

This morning she stood very still, closing her eyes after a while, and swaying. The salty breeze hit her upturned face. She licked her lips to taste it. A shudder of delight ran through her. For one split second she hardly breathed. Everything had melted together, the sun and the blue sky, the glittering ocean and rocks and wind, the wheeling gulls. Or was it that she had become a part of *them?*

"God?" she cried out hesitantly. "God, is that you?"

The sound of her own voice breaking the stillness made her giggle. Back in town, her friend Cheryl would probably scoff, "What a dumb idea!"

But it wasn't dumb. It was marvelous, and real. Yesterday the elderly pastor in the small country church on the hill had preached on the words of Psalm 136, "Whither shall I go from thy Spirit. . . ." The pastor's deep voice had rolled out the rest of the psalm but the only lines Ginny could remember were: "If I take the wings of the morning and dwell in the uttermost parts of the sea, even there thy hand shall lead me, . . ."

The minister had gone on to say something she'd found very interesting. The ancient Israelites, he explained, *shouted* their prayers of praise to the Lord. Shouted at the top of their lungs!

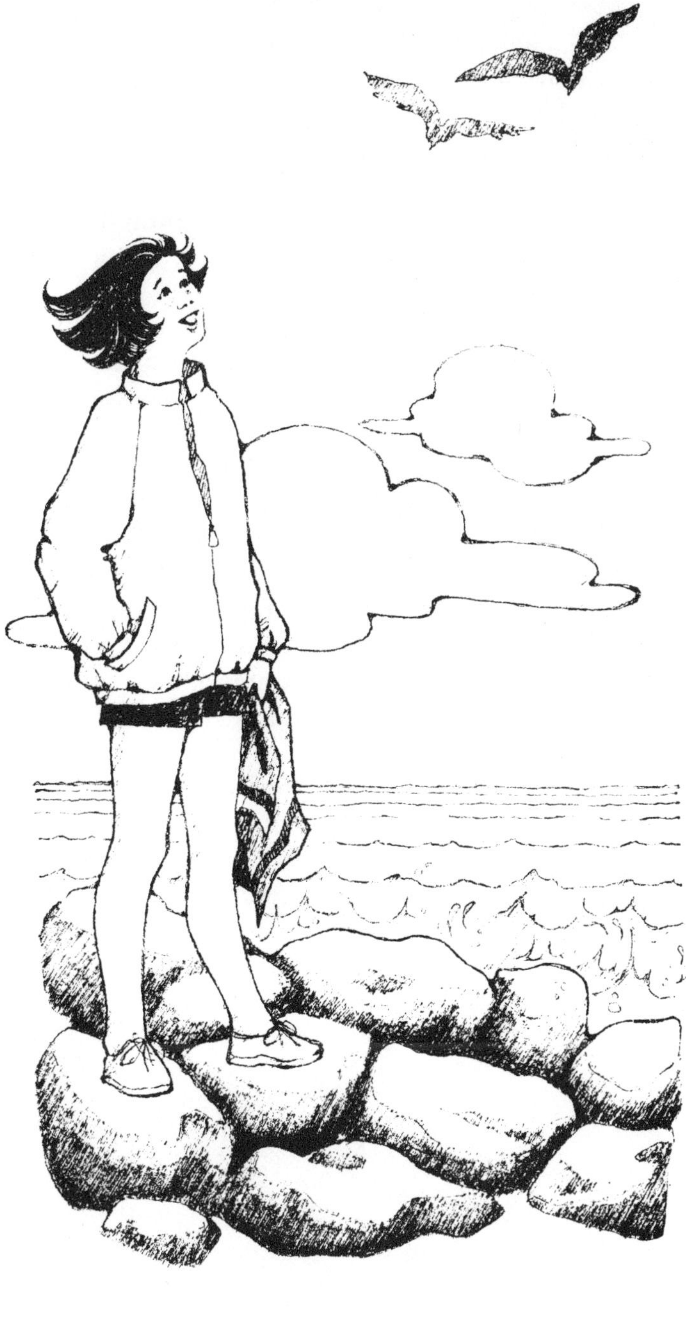

On the highest rock of the breakwater, arms akimbo, Ginny yelled, "Ayeeee Ooooh! Ayeeee Ooooh! You're here, God, I know it! I know it! Ayeeee Ooooh!"

She'd been away a long time. Mother and Dad would be worried. If she told them truthfully that she'd spent the time alone with God, would they believe her?

Quickly she climbed down from the rocks and hurried toward her family, first walking rapidly, then running and at last ending up with a series of cartwheels over and over down the beach.

As she went, she hollered in time with the cartwheels: "You're here, God! You're here! You're every . . . where, every . . . where, EVERYWHERE!"

> Make a joyful noise to the Lord, all the lands! Serve the Lord with gladness! Come into his presence with singing!
>
> Psalm 100:1-2

Heavenly Father, there are days when you are as close to me as my own breath or the rays of the sun. Quiet me, Lord, so these special moments may deepen my faith. Amen

Lord, I'm Back Again

Sometimes when I need God most he seems far away. Like when I'm alone in a scary place and I get frightened. Have I done something wrong to make it so I don't feel God's nearness?

"I love living here on the California coast," Bertie wrote in her letter to Sally. "I wish you weren't 3500 miles away though. Maybe your family can vacation here next summer. I'm sending a postcard so you can see how beautiful the beaches are."

She went on to tell Sally about the weird old house where she was baby-sitting. "The front steps sag and the paint is peeling, and the rambler rosebushes haven't been pruned back for years. But the Schrams, the people who bought it, are fixing it up."

Downstairs in the nursery Marvin and Nat were sound asleep. Mrs. Schram had told Bertie to feel free

17

to use her study in the tower to write letters. The door was open so she could hear the boys if they had a nightmare or cried.

She smoothed her paper and looked out the window, trying to remember the bits of news she'd saved to tell Sally. The storm was not over yet. In fact, the weather outside looked worse than it had when she'd practically floated through the front door two hours ago.

Tree branches lashed noisily against the streaming panes, making a sound like squeaky chalk. Downstairs a door banged. The Schrams must have left the door to the back porch open. She'd better check.

"Call me if you need me," Mother had said. "That's a spooky old house. Remember, Dad and I will be at the Grumbachers' after nine, but you can reach us there in an emergency."

At the time Bertie had grinned and said, "You know me, Mom. I don't scare easily."

And here she was, this very minute, shivering!

She tiptoed down the winding stairs to the second floor, past the bathroom with its high, old-fashioned tub. Mr. Schram had painted the funny feet on it gold. Mrs. Schram had warned her that Nat, the baby, was a fitful sleeper, so she did not bother to turn on the light in the long hall. She could hear Billy breathing snuffily as she passed the nursery. His mother had given him some cough medicine. No other sound. They were both fast asleep.

The next set of steps creaked eerily as she went down. My, but it was dark downstairs! This was the first time she'd been invited to baby-sit here. She had not noticed any light switch when she arrived. Now she fumbled around in the dark, trying to locate it but not having any luck.

She felt her way through the living room, hunting for either a lamp or a wall switch. She felt certain she had remembered to leave a light on before going up to put the little boys to bed. Yes, she distinctly remembered the hall light had been on. But it wasn't on now!

Her thoughts flew back to the sound of the door slamming. What if a stranger had come inside and was hiding some place? The very thought made her knees grow weak, her hands icy cold.

She stood in the darkened room filled with strange, lumpy shapes, trying to think what to do. She did not pray words out loud. Instead, in her mind, she thought a quick prayer, a jumble of words: "Lord, I've been asking you about all sorts of little things lately, I know, but this is something big. I'm truly frightened. I mean it, Lord, can you hear me?"

She'd known times when God seemed very close indeed. The evening her family had come upon the little house on Cottage Avenue was one of these occasions. They'd been staying outside of Gearhart in a motel while they househunted. Each of them had prayed about finding the right house. Finally, when time was running out, it was Daddy who had said calmly, "Let's leave the matter in God's hands. He'll take care of us."

Two days later, Mother shouted from the car, "Slow down, Henry, there it is—that house with blue shutters and a For Sale sign in front of it."

A shudder went through Bertie. "Lord, I'm back

again," she whispered. "If you hear me, please send me a signal."

Had she done something wrong? Was that why God was so far away tonight?

The ringing of the telephone made her jump. She followed the sound into the hall to the table near the staircase, wondering how she would manage to write down a message on the pad the Schrams had left for her.

It was Mrs. Schram!

"I'm glad you called," cried Bertie, trying not to sound too relieved. Then she decided Mrs. Schram might as well know the whole story.

"Please tell me where to turn on a light downstairs. I must have turned it off when I went up to the tower."

"You poor dear!" exclaimed Mrs. Schram. "I probably did it myself as I went out the front door. It's to the left of the door as you face the porch. There's a lamp in one corner of the living room, too, and a little reading light near the couch. How is everything?"

"Haven't heard a peep out of the boys," Bertie told her. "Mrs. Schram, did you leave a door open by mistake? I heard a bang when I was up in the tower."

Mrs. Schram chuckled. "I should have warned you. The bathroom window sometimes crashes down by itself. That's the next thing on our list to fix. We'll be home in an hour. I forgot to tell you there's cocoa in the cupboard and some leftover cupcakes in that pan on the stove. Help yourself."

"Thanks. I think I will." Bertie hung up the phone and turned on the hall light. She went into the living room and flicked the switch on the lamp near the couch.

She wasn't going to go back up in the tower, not yet. She was going to sit down here and enjoy the sounds of the rain and the wind. It felt cozy now, with the lights on. Cozy and safe.

She went out to the kitchen to warm a pot of cocoa. While she waited for it to be ready, she ate a couple of cupcakes. She was licking the chocolate icing off the third one when it came to her. God *had* sent a signal to let her know he was right there taking care of her. The telephone call—that was his signal!

"Lord, I'm back again," she said before she took another bite. "Thank you!"

> He who dwells in the shelter of the Most High, who abides in the shadow of the Almighty, will say to the Lord, "My refuge and my fortress; my God, in whom I trust."
>
> Psalm 91:1-2

God, whenever you seem far off, teach me how to recognize the signals you send to reassure me of your constant presence. Let me be certain that you will keep on caring for me, no matter what happens. Amen

It Looks Backwards, But Try It Anyway

When my friend does something that hurts me, why should I be the one to go ask her forgiveness? My Sunday school teacher says that's what the Bible tells us to do, but it sure looks backwards to me!

"Hi, Norma," said Mother when she walked in the door. Norma stomped down the tiny hall of the mobile home and into her bedroom without returning the greeting. She tossed her green knapsack on the chair and plopped down on her bed.

A tantalizing aroma drifted in from the kitchen. That was the one trouble with this place. Each room was so small that no matter where you were you could smell whatever Mother was cooking, and immediately you felt as hungry as a starving elephant.

Today the smell of fresh cherry pie was tempting. Determined not to weaken, Norma kicked the door shut before she opened the crumpled paper in her hand.

> Norma Grout
> Will always pout
> Whenever her friends
> Begin to shout:
> "Norma Jean is *dreadfully* stout!"

"That Gloria Freebolt! I'll never speak to her again!" sputtered Norma. "What a stupid thing to write about someone you've lived next door to for three years!"

An image of Gloria's thin figure swam hazily before her. Who wanted to be as skinny as a scarecrow?

"You're *scrawny!*" she burst out angrily.

"*Who* is?" asked a voice.

Norma looked up in surprise at her older brother. "Bill Grout, it's none of your business! Shut up and leave me alone."

"Sorry. I was only trying to help," said Bill. He backed out of the room holding his piece of cherry pie carefully so the sticky red juice would not run off the plate.

Norma heard him go into the cubbyhole of a bedroom next to hers. When he set the plate down on his desk, his fork clattered to the floor. Presently there was a thump and the sound of a desk drawer opening. A sophomore at Baxter High, Bill had piles of homework to do each night.

His transistor radio blared, but she didn't bother to rap on the wall to get him to turn it down. She wished he hadn't waved the cherry pie under her nose.

Norma opened her own desk drawer to find a sheet

of scrap paper. "Gloria Freebolt, watch out!" She was pretty good at rhyming herself. But what could anyone in the entire world do with either *Gloria* or *Freebolt?*

Folding the paper in half down the middle, she scribbled *Gloria* at the head of one column and *Freebolt* across the top of the other.

Half an hour later the paper was still blank. Her stomach made a funny noise, announcing it was ready for at least a small wedge of pie and maybe a glass of milk.

As Norma hesitated, a few words spilled onto the paper, practically by themselves:

> Gloria's hair is stringy and brown;
> She's thin as a bag of bones.

Neither line was true, of course. Gloria had the kind of hair people were always raving about, a rich, glossy brown and naturally curly. And her figure was good too.

"But then, I'm not stout, either," thought Norma, reading the lines she had written and frowning. The doctor told me I was only four pounds overweight when I went in for my camp physical. And he said I'd probably look about right when I grew another inch or two.

What rhymed with *brown* and *bones?* She chewed her pencil eraser into crumbly bits, but no fresh words popped out. She'd have to finish the verse later and stick it in Gloria's desk the first thing tomorrow morning. Sadly she took aim and spat the eraser crumbs into her trash basket.

Writing awful things about Gloria had only made matters worse. She sat there a while thinking of the things they'd done together—roller skating and swimming; bike riding down Deadman's Hill. Gloria was the only kid brave enough to do that with her. And she was one of the few children from school who lived here in the mobile home park. It would be lonesome now that they weren't going to be friends anymore.

Norma reached for a tissue. She wasn't crying but her eyes felt a little damp. She dried them and blew her nose before going out to the kitchen.

Mother had left for her evening shift at the little grocery store at the edge of the park. Ah, there was the pie on the counter with a hasty note beside it: You kids leave enough for dessert, please.

Someone was rapping on the door. It was Jake, the youth leader from church. He glanced hungrily at the pie.

Norma's mouth twitched. "Wait; I'll cut you a piece."

"I can stay just a minute or two," he said. "I came by to leave this material for your mother. She offered to sub for me on Sunday evening at youth group. I'll be at a conference."

Norma sat down on the couch with her feet tucked under her. She looked over at Jake, stretched comfortably in one of the big chairs with his feet on the hassock.

"Jake, I've got a question I don't want to ask in our discussion group. Especially if my own mother is leading it next time."

Amusement flickered in his eyes. He swallowed a bite of pie. "Go ahead, then, shoot," he said agreeably. "I'm ready for anything."

"This one's hard. You know how we talked about forgiving people a couple of Sunday nights ago? And you read us that verse from the Bible, the one that sounds so backwards?"

"Mmmm hmmm. The one that says if your brother has wronged you, don't wait for him to come and apologize. You go to *him* and fix things up instead."

"Well, I've discovered something," Norma burst out. "That's a real dumb idea. It won't work."

There was a long silence as Jake scraped up the last of his pie and licked the fork. "Marvelous pie," he said. He handed her the empty plate. "How do you know it won't work, Norma? You've got me curious. Have you tried it recently?"

She shook her head. "Nooo . . ." she admitted slowly. "And I'm not going to either."

He turned to her before bounding down the steps in front of the mobile home. "You might change your mind," he remarked with a smile. "The last time *I* tried it, know what happened? It worked! Nobody was more surprised than I was. I'll tell you the story another time if you remind me. Right now I've got an appointment at the church."

Norma set the dirty plates in the sink and ran some water on them. In her bedroom she picked up the scribbled piece of paper and stared at it for a few minutes. Suddenly she ripped it in half, ran out the front door and down the steps, and over to the sage green mobile home in the next lot.

She did not know what she was going to say if Gloria answered the door. But she had no time to think—the door flew open and there she was, looking cute and giggly in a frayed pair of blue jean cut-offs and a plaid shirt.

"Am I ever glad to see you!" she cried, tugging Norma into the mobile home. "I didn't think you'd ever speak to me again. I don't know what got into me, Norma."

They were in her bedroom now, a bedroom smaller than the one Norma had next door because Gloria's father had lined the walls with shelves to hold her stuffed animal collection. Panda bears and hippopotamuses and mice and rabbits and dogs of various sizes were crowded haphazardly onto the shelves.

"I felt mean too," Norma told her.

"But I was the one who started it. I'm sorry, honest I am," said Gloria. "I was going to bring this over and stick it in your mailbox."

She handed Norma a paper neatly lettered with colored felt pens:

> Norma Grout
> I'd like to shout
> What our friendship's
> All about.
> The fun we have,
> The things we do,
> I'm glad I know
> Someone like you!

"Remember the first time your brother took us bowling?" she asked.

Norma nodded. "I dropped the ball on your foot. And what about the time we explored the pioneer schoolhouse on Sudbury Road?"

"Those awful noises!" exclaimed Gloria giggling.

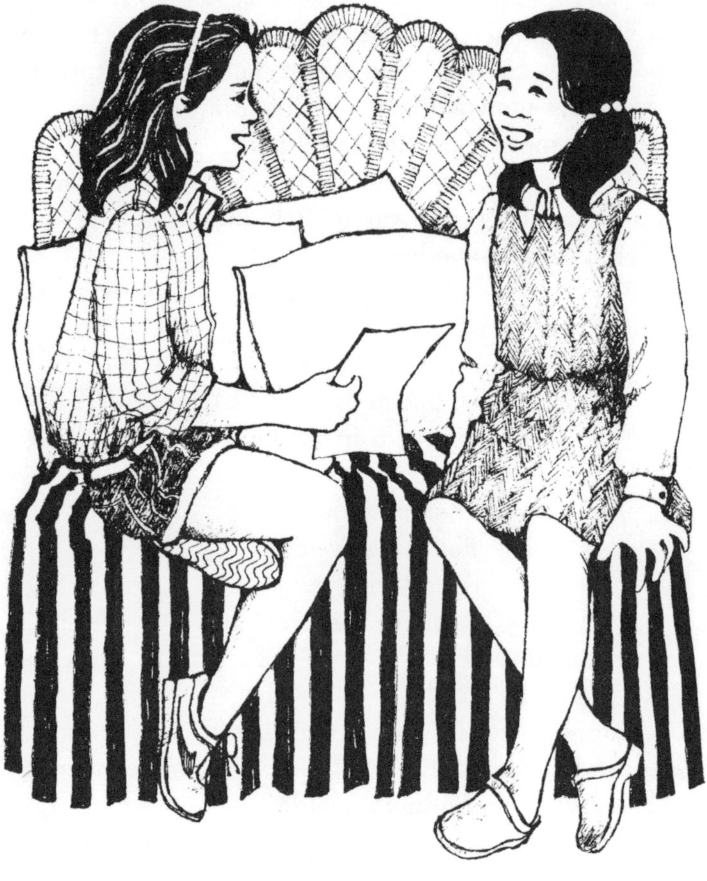

"Scritchy-scratchy, scritchy-scratchy. And it was nothing but field mice!"

"Now that spring is here we could ride our bikes out there for a picnic," suggested Norma. "How about next Saturday?"

"How about the week after that instead?" asked Gloria. "My family is going over to the beach this weekend and I was going to ask my mother if you could go along. I'm sure she'll say it's OK."

Norma glanced out the bedroom door at the clock on the living room wall. "Oops, it's after six. I've got to go home and warm up the casserole Mom left for Bill and me. But first I'll stop by the store and tell her about your invitation."

Gloria grinned as she handed her the new verse she had written. "Don't forget this. Hang it on your bulletin board as a reminder—we're still friends."

> So if you are offering your gift at the altar, and there remember that your brother has something against you, leave your gift there before the altar and go; first be reconciled to your brother, and then come and offer your gift.
>
> Matthew 5:23-24

Jesus, give me the nerve to walk the way you showed your disciples, even when it seems exactly the opposite of what I want to do. Teach me how to forgive the people who hurt me. Amen

I Feel So Different

I feel so different. I'm not good in gym. Some of the equipment scares me. And kids tease me when I throw a ball left-handed. What I really like to do is write stories. Will I always feel like an oddball?

"Have you ever watched her throw a ball? I s'pose it's because she's a southpaw, but she's a scream."

"Well, I know one thing. She's scared to death to climb the ropes in gym."

Delsie and Sue didn't realize Sandra had heard every word of their conversation. Quickly she slipped out of her gym shorts, grabbed her towel, and vanished into the shower. She stood waiting for the first rush of cold water to warm up.

They were right. Of all the gym equipment, the dangling ropes scared her most. If only she had a good excuse to remain at the bottom. Not that she'd want to trade places with Jackie, the girl with the back brace who was allowed to take an extra hour of home ec instead of gym.

Still thinking about it, Sandra soaped, rinsed, toweled herself dry, and put on her jeans and the new striped top she and Mom had bought the other day.

She strolled past Delsie and Sue, pretending they didn't exist. For a fleeting moment, before leaving the locker room, she stared into the full-length mirror on the back of the door.

She *looked* like everyone else, didn't she? She wore the same style of clothing—jeans, shirts, tennis shoes. She ate the same foods, except for chocolate. She only skipped that because it made her pimples worse. Her short blonde hair was naturally curly.

She pinched her arm. "I'm real," she thought unhappily. "Just like everyone else in this school. Why do I feel like such an oddball?"

In social studies they were studying the ancient Greek culture. Usually it was interesting because she enjoyed reading about long-ago times. But today it seemed dull. She had read two chapters ahead in the textbook and had completed the written assignments for the week. Her paper was going to be about her favorite myths. That she loved doing, but the project was home in her desk drawer.

Never mind; she could pretend she was hard at work. She often did that. And then she'd begin to imagine different stories: ghost stories, mysteries, stories about a cat named Dicky who had wonderful adventures. Lately Dicky had taken a plane trip to Florida and was seeking a way back to New Jersey.

Did cats ever walk that far? Once Sandra had read

a story about a cat that found its way home by walking nearly 200 miles. But in real life?

As she wrote a new story, she made a list in the margin of her loose-leaf paper of words she might want to use, words with nice sounds and ones that painted pictures as she said them to herself: rip, gummy, plum-colored, sly, wink, bleary, glimmer.

The buzzer jolted her back to the present. Math was next and she needed to concentrate on it. Her story would have to wait until late afternoon when she could climb her Thinking Tree to finish it.

She could hardly wait. It was a good story, this one. She could tell by the way the words flowed out. It was strange, though—sometimes the opposite was true. When a story was difficult to write she did it over and over until at last it pleased her. And, in the end, she'd come up with something fine.

Grandpa, the only person she'd ever allowed to read her stories, said it was like sanding the roughness from the wooden figures he carved.

He was outside when she got home, pruning the shrubbery and waiting for her. "Your ma took the car for a tune-up. Said to be sure to let you know there's some lemon pudding in the refrigerator. How'd things go today, Sandy?"

Sandra shrugged. "I guess I don't like school that much, Gramps. I don't mind the work. It's . . . it's the kids. None of them seem to like the same kinds of things I do and it gets lonesome."

She went inside to get the pudding. In a few minutes she returned with two custard cups full of it and a handful of cookies. She gave one cup to her grandfather.

Side by side they sat on the front steps. "What I don't understand is how I want to be like everyone else and yet I still like to be by myself a lot of the time. How can a person want two things at once, Gramps?"

"There's a difference between being lonely and being alone," he told her. He spoke slowly, between bites of cookie and pudding, jabbing the air with his spoon to drive his point home.

"Take me, Sandy. All my life I've loved to be by myself, doing the gardening, working on the small wheat farm your grandma and I used to own. She knew that, and let me be. But we shared a lot, you know. Early in the morning we'd read the Bible together. We did that every day until she died. Forty-one years. Sometimes in the summer, when the working day was long, it was only a few verses or a psalm and a prayer. And then, in the evening, she'd have a hot bath ready when I came in tired and dusty. After a good meal, she'd read the newspaper to me and we'd talk about things." His voice trembled. "I don't mind being alone, you see. But I do get lonely now that she's gone."

"Why, that's the way I feel too!" exclaimed Sandra. "Thanks, Gramps. There's a story I want to finish before I forget the . . . ."

Her grandfather patted her shoulder and said gently, "Hold your horses. I've got something I want to share with you before you climb that tree of yours."

He went into the house and came out lugging his big Bible and a magnifying glass.

Secretly Sandra loved that old Bible. She liked the musty smell, the worn black leather covers with

33

the gilt words on the front, the tissue-thin pages, and the place in the middle where family records had been written over the years. The thing she enjoyed most, though, was the way Gramps, and perhaps Grandma too, had marked their favorite verses with a pencil. In several places dates had been written in the wide outer margins. When asked, Grandpa had explained that whenever happy or sad or difficult experiences had come their way, they had marked the date by the verse that seemed most helpful.

Today he turned to 1 Peter 4:10 and read to Sandra: "As each has received a gift, employ it for one another, as good stewards of God's varied grace."

"God gave me a gift," he said in a voice as quiet as the breeze rippling softly through the cottonwood tree. He pushed a shock of white hair out of his eyes. "He gave me a way with the earth. I've tried to take care of his gift, be a steward of it and use it properly for the family and others." He looked sideways at his granddaughter to see if she was listening. Satisfied he had her full attention, he went on. "Yours is a special gift, Sandra, this gift with words. Maybe (he pronounced it 'mebbe') you'll grow up to write a book that will change somebody's life. Goodness knows I've read many a book that had an effect on *me!*"

He laid his bony hand lightly on her knee. She gazed at the wrinkles and creases, the blunt, yellowed fingernails, knowing he had more to say. "Yes, Grandpa?"

"Don't be afraid of your gift," he remarked a little gruffly. "So you feel different than the others. No harm in that, Sandy. Be a good steward of it and *share* it too." His eyes crinkled as if he might be holding back a smile. "You're not the only kid who likes to write, you know. I wouldn't be surprised if you discovered two or three others like yourself."

"Thanks, Gramps. I feel *much* better now." She turned to kiss him on the cheek before running off to her Thinking Tree to finish the story.

> But each has his own special gift from God, one of one kind and one of another.
>
> 1 Corinthians 7:7b

Heavenly Father, thank you for giving me a gift I enjoy using. I need to discover ways to share it with others. Let me never be afraid to be myself, the person you've made me, and not a copy of anyone else. Amen

The Unanswered Question

I'm the only one in our family who goes to church. My father died last year and Mom and my older sister and brother like to sleep in and have a late breakfast on Sunday. What will happen to them if they never find out about God? I think Mom would feel less lonesome if she'd come sometimes.

When the Walgrams' horn beeped, Sharon zipped her jacket, pulled her hood up to protect her hair from the snow which had fallen steadily for nearly a day, and hurried out the door.

If the doorbell rang, Mom and Neil and Helen would wake up. Helen, at least, would be very cross. She had worked late at the hospital, helping to deliver a baby.

"Hi," Mr. Walgram greeted her with a cheery smile.

In the back seat of the van, Fern kept tight hold on her baby sister and slid toward the window to make room. Sharon climbed in.

"We're early because of the special choir practice," explained Mrs. Walgram looking back. "Fern was supposed to remind you."

"I don't like to bug people," said Fern. "Sharon, let's stay and play in the nursery when we take Kelly. It won't be so boring waiting for Sunday school to begin."

Sharon smiled. It was queer to think how different they were even though they were the best of friends. Fern didn't like Sunday school and church very much. But to Sharon, St. Matthew's Church was a delightful place, full of people rushing around laughing and talking, nice music, and a quiet time to think about things while the pastor talked. During the week there were potlucks and trips, choir practices for children and adults, and different kinds of meetings.

On a regular Sunday like today, there would be Sunday school followed by the service in the big church. Sometimes, instead of the organ, a group of guitar players accompanied the people when they sang.

While Mr. Walgram parked the car, Sharon followed Fern and her mother into church. Mrs. Walgram carried the baby along the slippery walk. At the door she handed Kelly to Fern saying, "See you two at the coffee hour."

Fern and Sharon knew they'd see her sooner than that, marching up the aisle in her long blue choir robe.

"Good morning, girls," said Pastor Ewald. He never

forgot to say "Hi" no matter how many things were on his mind.

"Hello, Fern! Hello, Sharon!" That was Mrs. Dahl waving. She and her husband were the superintendents of the Sunday school, one heading the upper classes and one the primary division. Sharon waved back before following Fern into the "baby room."

"I'd rather be outside playing in the snow," sighed Fern. She dumped Kelly into a nursery crib and handed her bottle of milk to Elsie, the teenager in charge.

"Only give it to her if she cries," she told Elsie. She giggled. "She's getting pudgy, isn't she?"

"We'll have the entire afternoon to play," said Sharon. "Anyway, Tom Bradford says there's a movie in Sunday school today, before we break into our classes.

The movie was about the boat people who were on their way to America. St. Matthew's Church was sponsoring one of these families. The girls could hardly wait for them to arrive. Only a few weeks were left to help the grown-ups work on the apartment that had been rented for them. Pastor's letter stated there would be a grandmother, a grandfather, an older son, two teenage boys, a girl about 11, a baby, and the mother. Eight people who had had such a difficult time that the father had died along the way.

The family coming to St. Matthews was Cambodian but the people in the movie had come from many places in East Asia. Mrs. Dahl reminded the Sunday school to keep on collecting clothing in small sizes, because the family members would be quite short and thin. The 11-year-old girl, for instance, would probably be able to wear a size 10 from the children's department.

"That makes it hard," whispered Fern. "My cousin could give her some nice tops, but they look as though they're for little kids."

Later, sitting between Mr. Walgram and Fern in church, Sharon tried to picture what the family would be like. Volunteers at the East Asian Center downtown would tutor them in English, and so would members of the church. Sharon and Fern had offered to baby-sit free sometimes so the family would be able to go to the center.

A sharp nudge interrupted her thoughts. Fern was inviting her to play tic-tac-toe on the edge of the church bulletin. Sharon grinned at her friend and shook her head no. Fern was the kind of girl who jumped and tumbled and bounced almost everyplace she went. She hated to sit still in school or church. Of course, in school she got to move around to the gym and home ec room and the media center and that helped some.

Sharon enjoyed outdoor activities too. But for the time being she was content to listen to the singing and gaze at the colored stained-glass windows. She liked the windows with the most blue in them the best, especially the one of the Wise Men laying their gifts at the feet of the baby Jesus.

Mother would like this church if she'd try coming once. As soon as Mom had heard about the boat family, she had set aside a box of clean clothing. Now she was knitting a tiny sweater for the baby.

But whenever Sharon invited her to come to

church, she said, "Sunday is the only day of the week I can sleep in. Remember, I have to work half-days on Saturday. Besides, as long as I do my best and show concern for others, what difference does it make if I believe in Jesus Christ or attend church?"

That question bothered Sharon a lot. Sometimes at night when she was in bed thinking about Daddy and how he'd never be there again to beat her at Ping-Pong or to help with her math problems, that question rang in her ears.

Mother really didn't want an answer. She seemed content the way she was, proud to be supporting the family with her income, proud that nobody ever saw her cry except the night of Daddy's death.

For Sharon, the bits and pieces she heard in church about Jesus and the kingdom of heaven did make a difference. She was beginning to sense that she wouldn't always feel so bad about things that had happened, like Daddy's long sickness and his death. Gradually the pain would lessen. That would be true for the Cambodian family after they got settled too.

But there was another part to the question. She felt shy about asking Pastor Ewald, yet someday she was determined she would be brave enough to knock on his study door and ask: "What happens to the millions of kind, good people like my mom and dad and the rest of my family, and the boat people who haven't been converted to Christianity, when they die? If they don't go to heaven, where do they go?"

The organ rang out with the chords of *A Mighty Fortress Is Our God.* Mr. Walgram smiled as Sharon jerked into the present. Goodness, church was almost over!

"You look as though you've been far away in another land," he joshed her as they filed out.

"I was," admitted Sharon. "I was doing my thinking."

"Church is a good place for that," he said.

"Mostly it was about a question that has been on my mind," Sharon told him shyly. "About people who don't come to church or believe Jesus was God's Son."

"Here's the very person who can help," commented Mr. Walgram. He reached out to shake Pastor Ewald's hand. Then he leaned forward so the rest of the people could not hear what he was saying. "Pastor, this young friend of mine, Sharon, has a question. Whatever it is, I'm sure you can help her."

For a minute or two, right there in the lobby of the church, the pastor held up the line of people streaming out while he said, "There's no time like the present for dealing with questions. How about dropping by my study after coffee hour?" He turned to Mr. Walgram. "You and your family can go on, Jack. I'll see that Sharon gets home."

Sharon was so surprised she felt tongue-tied. But she had time during the coffee hour to think of what she wanted to say. After everyone else had left, she took a deep breath and followed Pastor Ewald's stocky figure into the study. She looked around at the walls lined with books. Pretty soon she found herself talking about many things—her father's illness, and the way she felt waking up and knowing she'd never hear his deep voice and funny, rumbling laugh again. She told him about Mom and how she'd heard her crying behind the closed bedroom door.

At last she got around to her question. "Pastor, I've

41

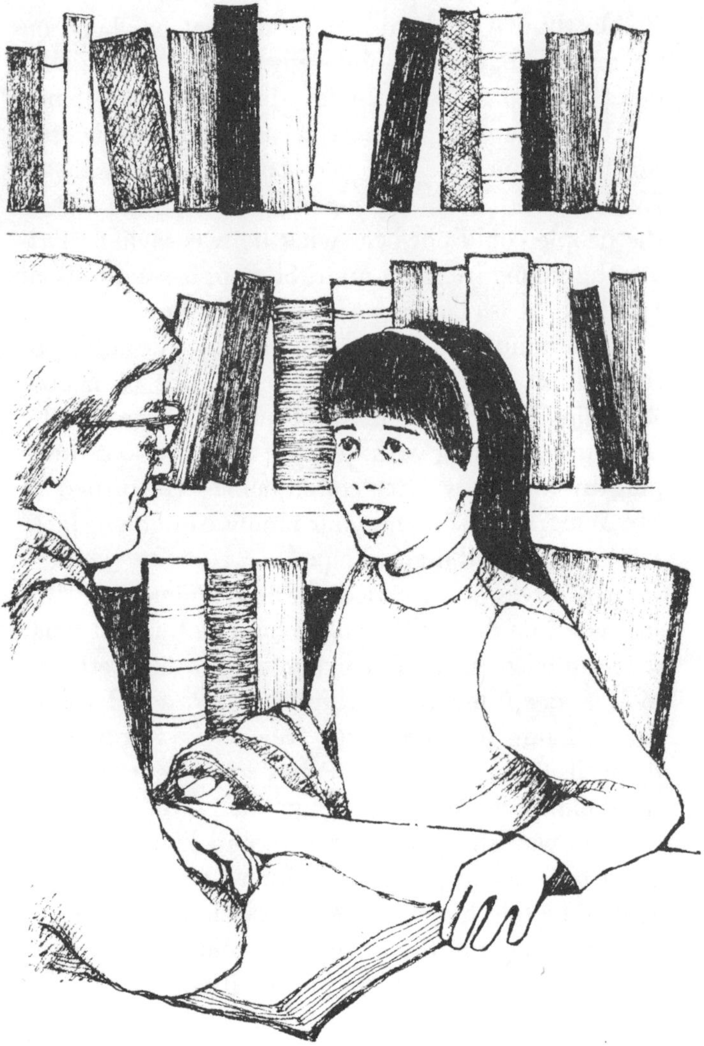

been wondering about heaven," she began. "My father never went to church and Mom doesn't want to come . . ." she paused.

"Most of the rest of the world doesn't either," he added gently.

"Some of the kindest people I know don't seem to have any . . . any definite kind of belief in God or Jesus." Sharon's voice faltered. "Pastor, if my father isn't in heaven with God, *where is he?*" She glanced over at the books again. "You've read hundreds of books so you probably know the answer."

"Ah, but I don't," he said. The eyes beneath the steel gray eyebrows twinkled as he continued, but his face was as sober as if he were discussing a matter of great importance with Mr. or Mrs. Walgram.

"The ways of God are far beyond what our little human minds can understand, Sharon. The prophet Isaiah says it someplace in slightly different words. But the verse I like best when I think of my unconverted friends—and I have many—is in Ezekiel, one of the books of the Old Testament."

He pivoted in his chair so he could reach his Bible from the shelf. "Listen to this. It's from the 34th chapter, verses 15 and 16, if you want to look it up again later:

> I myself will be the shepherd of my sheep, and I will make them lie down, says the Lord God. I will seek the lost, and I will bring back the strayed, and I will bind up the crippled, and I will strengthen the weak, and the fat and the strong I will watch over; I will feed them in justice.

Sharon smiled. "It sounds like the Bible is telling us to leave those complicated things to God."

"Exactly," said the pastor. "We need to learn how to trust that our loved ones are in his hands, and let him seek the lost and bring back the strayed in his own way and in his own time." He chuckled. "Often God seems to work slowly, but there is one thing we can do. We can go on praying for the people in the world who don't know him."

He snapped the Bible shut and put it back on the shelf. "Now if you are ready, I'll give you a lift home. Be sure to stop by any time you want to discuss questions with me."

"Thanks," said Sharon.

Side by side, they walked down the long flight of stairs and out into the falling snow to the pastor's car.

> For as the heavens are higher than the earth, so are my ways higher than your ways and my thoughts than your thoughts.
> Isaiah 55:9

Dear God, sometimes your ways are hard to understand and sometimes there are no answers to my questions. Lord of the universe, help me to be patient and to trust you. Amen

Mixed Messages

My parents yell and argue with one another. I'm afraid that pretty soon they'll come to me to tell me they're getting a divorce. Yet sometimes they hug each other and say nice things. I'm mixed up. I wish I could ask them about it.

Mother and Dad were at it again. Mary Ann heard their voices arguing back and forth the minute she opened the door of the fifth floor apartment. This time it seemed to be a squabble over who would get to use the car tomorrow. On the days Dad drove to the office, Mom had to get up real early to go to her classes by bus. She was studying to become a physical therapist and the college she went to was clear on the other side of town.

"I can't help it. I didn't *ask* you to go back to

school, did I?" Mary Ann heard her father say in an angry voice.

"You'll be happy enough when we have two salary checks coming in," retorted Mother. She spoke shrilly, as she always did when annoyed. "We never should have sold the old Plymouth. I could've driven Mary Ann to school and then hopped right over to the college...."

"Oh, come off it," interrupted Daddy. Soon he lowered his voice so that all his eavesdropping daughter could hear was "mumble mumble mumble."

"Mumble mumble mumble," answered Mother.

Had they realized she was home from school? Guiltily Mary Ann clattered into the kitchen so they'd be sure to know. First she peered into the clown-shaped cookie jar and, finding it empty, turned to the refrigerator. Her stomach felt as if it had been twisted somehow. Food might make her throw up. She settled for a glass of cold pineapple juice and sat on a kitchen stool to gulp it down.

If only Dena were here; Dena would know how to make things all right again. But her older sister had been married for over a year. She was busy building a home in Ferndale with Greg.

The voices started in again, this time they were quite loud. Mary Ann hurried into the bedroom. Dena's white bed was there, across the room from her own. She knelt on hands and knees to hunt for her comfortable old tennis shoes with knotted laces and thin soles. Next she wrote a note to Mom, letting her know she was off on a shopping spree with her friend Roberta. She had promised to help Roberta select a birthday gift for her little brother Kevin.

bed is still in your room. We can talk all night."

"I'll cut my evening class," decided Mom. "I'll call my friend Jan and ask her to tape the lecture."

"Luckily this is the one night of the week I'm free," put in Dad.

Because Dena was home again, they seemed to be in good spirits, Mary Ann noticed wistfully. Everything was the way it had been before she went away; people laughing and talking, bumping into one another in the small kitchen as everyone helped Mom put dinner on the table.

Mom had had the time to bake Dena's favorite chicken and noodle casserole. As the meal progressed, Mary Ann grew quiet. She looked around the table at the smiling faces. Mom and Dad were putting on a great act. Dena didn't seem to suspect anything.

"Mary Ann, you're dreaming again. You've done that a lot lately. Please finish your dinner." Mother was speaking to her, but Mary Ann noticed she shot a peculiar look at Dena.

"I'm not hungry," said Mary Ann. "Roberta and I ate caramel apples on the way home."

"You'd better eat some for energy if you two are planning to stay up and gab," teased Daddy.

He was acting so nice—it made Mary Ann choke on her next bite. Hadn't Roberta said that was the way her parents had behaved right before they split up?

Once she and Dena were alone in the bedroom, Mary Ann didn't know where to begin. She thought of several different ways while she brushed her teeth. Not one of them seemed right. She hopped into bed and lay there watching her sister brush her dark hair to a glossy shine.

"Remember how we used to say a prayer together?" asked Dena as she brushed. "Shall we do it tonight, for old times sake?"

Mary Ann shook her head. "Not yet. Let's talk awhile. Tell me about your new house, Dena." That wasn't what she'd expected to say, but somehow the worrisome thoughts stayed buried deep inside.

Dena turned around and caught her completely by surprise. "Mary Ann, what's wrong? Tell me. You and I have always been able to share. Did you guess why Mom and Dad called me and begged me to spend a few days here? They're concerned about you, Sis. You've gotten so pale and quiet, so unlike the bubbly Mary Ann they used to know."

"What's wrong with *me?*" cried Mary Ann indignantly. "Dena, it's *them.* They argue all the time and everything has gotten so . . . so strained. Both Mom and Dad look dreadfully tired. They . . . they try to hide it behind that closed bedroom door, but they can't fool me. I know they're headed for a divorce and aren't going to tell me until it's final. My friend Roberta says that's the way her folks acted too. She . . . she . . . ," Mary Ann slowed down, trying to recall Roberta's parting shot. "She said, 'It sounds like bad news.'"

"Not to me," declared Dena. Unexpectedly she began to laugh. When her laugh turned to a side-splitting roar, Mary Ann grew alarmed, but her sister's laughter was so contagious that she found herself joining in, although she didn't know why. It was silly to be laughing when she wanted to cry.

"Look," said Dena, with an air of authority. "Maybe I've only been married for a year. But I know all about this. It's nothing but a case of mixed messages. Mom and Dad are frightfully tired. You're right about that. And they don't have much time to spend together or with you. Their routine is upset. It makes them cranky. But," she grinned at Mary Ann, "what distresses them more than anything else is the way you've changed. You used to be such a peppy, happy-go-lucky girl."

She began to laugh again. "Oh, it's all so funny! You see, they don't know yet that *you've* been worried about *them* and that's why you're so blue these days."

Dena glanced at the small alarm clock she had sent her younger sister for Christmas. "It's only 11 o'clock. They won't be asleep yet and we need to go in and clear up this mess right now."

Mother and Daddy were propped against the pillows in the big bed. Dad was deep in a new science fiction paperback, and Mom was working on a crossword puzzle.

When the girls knocked, she called, "Come in." And then: "What's a six-letter word for a body of water?"

"Never mind that. What's a five-letter word for mistake?" asked Dena. "*Mix-up*, that's what it is." She laughed at her mother's puzzled expression.

"You and Daddy and Mary Ann have been completely mixed up about one another," Dena went on.

"I'll say!" chimed in Mary Ann. "Now put away that puzzle and the science fiction book and listen."

"We used to eat supper together," remarked Dad when the girls were finished. "But it's harder to do that now, with these different schedules."

"I wouldn't mind waiting until eight o'clock to eat

51

with you and Mom," suggested Mary Ann. "It gets lonesome eating by myself."

"We could try getting up early enough to have breakfast together," said Mom. "That way we might share our plans for the day. Perhaps if we think things through and do some rearranging and sharing we won't be giving each other mixed messages anymore."

"I know I have to work on that temper of mine," added Dad. "It does get out of control far too easily."

Mother smiled. "I'll do my best to count to 10 before I shriek out some idiotic answer. Part of it is plain bad habit." She put her arm around her youngest daughter. "Mary Ann, perhaps your father and I *have* been too tense and out of sorts lately. We certainly have argued a lot. But we love one another. Remember that, dear. There is room for disagreements and arguing in marriage as long as both wife and husband are sure of one another's love."

"I guess I have something to work on too," admitted Mary Ann with a yawn. "Next time I'm unsure about the way things are going, I'll ask you first instead of picturing the way it might be. Dena, let's go back to bed. We've got some catching up to do.

> Hatred stirs up strife, but love covers all offenses.
> Proverbs 10:12

Show me the way to have an open and honest relationship with members of my family, Lord. Please strengthen our love for one another with your love. Sometimes we get angry with each other. Then help us learn how to let love wipe away the pain. Amen

Surprise! Surprise!

My friends want me to join in a mean prank on Halloween. It sounds like fun, but I know it would be wrong. I need to have the courage to say no.

"Every Halloween that old Mr. Straub does the same thing," complained Meg. "All the other neighbors let us choose from plates full of cookies and apples. But not Mr. Straub."

"I think he's stingy," said Fran. "This time it would be fun to play a trick on the old skinflint. Last year he turned his lights off early and went to bed. I don't see why he has to be such a spoilsport."

"Serve him right if we soap his windows!" declared Julie.

"My brother Glenn will help us do it," added Ruth Ellen. Her eyes sparkled mischievously. "But I've thought of a better plan. Let's get Glenn and his friend Skip to help us stick Mr. Straub's porch furniture up on that low roof that juts out at the side of his house. There'll be two of us to be lookouts and three to do the job."

Julie glanced around at her friends. They were sprawled on the living room carpet at Ruth Ellen's house, munching a bowl of granola and drinking the pitcher of fruit punch her mom had made for them.

"It sounds more exciting than collecting bags full of candy," she admitted slowly. "We're getting kind of big for that anyway. I was planning to take my little brother and sister around to a few houses. But I guess either Mom or Dad would be willing to walk with them instead."

What would her parents say if they got wind of the plan they were cooking up here at Ruth Ellen's house? It didn't matter. If she were careful, they'd never find out. It wasn't as if this were going to be a cruel trick. The kids only wanted to tease Mr. Straub a little, to pay him back for being so mean.

"Tomorrow's Sunday," she went on. "My family will be busy with church and then we're going to carve our jack-o'-lanterns and set them out on the porch rail. See you in school on Monday. That's Halloween!"

"We'll make sure Glenn and Skip are in on the plan," Meg called after her. "Don't you forget about it, Julie. Better hunt up a flashlight with good batteries."

Julie scuffed home through piles of gold and scarlet leaves, picturing the surprise on Mr. Straub's face when he woke up and discovered his wicker porch furniture was on his roof.

The lights were off in the huge white corner house where the old man lived. Usually he was sitting outside at dusk, in one of the green chairs, watching everything that went on in the neighborhood. Tonight there was no sign of him.

She frowned, remembering the time little Jamie's ball had landed in Mr. Straub's petunia bed. Jamie had been too timid to ring the doorbell and ask if he could look for it. And when Julie had hunted the next day, the ball was gone. "He probably threw it away," she had told Jamie. "He's like that; a real crabby person."

Then there was the time he had hollered at Nan who was only four. Apparently Nan had ridden her trike up Mr. Straub's walk. She came home sobbing, "I—I don't know why he yelled . . . he j-just did."

"He's an old man who doesn't seem to enjoy children," Mom had comforted her.

"But that doesn't give him the right to scare little kids," Julie had protested angrily.

Tonight Mom was putting the finishing touches on the kids' costumes when Julie walked in.

"Oh, Julie, look at me, I'm a clown," cried Jamie.

"And I'm Cinderella," shouted Nan, dancing around the living room with her gold cardboard crown tipping into her eyes. "Are you going to be a witch again, Julie? You looked real, but you didn't fool me."

"I'll see," promised Julie.

Hearing the doubt in her voice, Mother looked up. She stuck a pin in the hem of Nan's blue princess gown before saying, "The witch costume is on the bottom shelf of the hall cupboard if you want it,

55

Julie. It was large on you last year so I believe it will still fit."

"Mom," said Julie, "do you suppose you could take the kids trick or treating instead of me? Meg and Ruth Ellen want me to spend Halloween with them. We're getting kind of big to go around in costumes."

"But not too grown up to carve a jack-o'-lantern, I hope," called her father from the kitchen where he was slicing the ham for Mom.

Julie laughed. "I'll never be too old for that."

Later in the evening, Meg called. "We've rounded up the boys," she informed Julie. "And we've decided to give Mr. Straub one chance. It'll be a real trick or treat. If he does answer the door and hand out stuff, we'll forget about the trick part. OK?"

"OK," said Julie. She knew, and the others knew too, that Mr. Straub would not have a plate of treats ready.

Several times on Sunday and during school on Monday, when she remembered the trick she and her friends were going to play on Mr. Straub, the back of her neck prickled uncomfortably.

Mother and Dad might not know what she was up to, but there was no way to fool God. And if she changed her mind, the other kids would say she "chickened out."

She was surprised, coming home from school after band practice, when she turned the corner onto Michigan Street and saw her own mother hurrying down the walk of Mr. Straub's house in the dusk.

"Wait up, Julie," her mom called. "Could you possibly change your plans and take the little ones out to a few houses tonight? Your father is on evening shift at the post office, and I've discovered that poor old Mr. Straub is in the hospital. It seems he sprained his ankle late Saturday, or thought he did. Today the doctor discovered a hairline fracture. His foot is swollen and they're keeping him at the hospital for at least a week."

As Julie stood on the sidewalk, lost in thought, her mother continued, "The nurse called to see if I would drop by and get his key from him so I could go feed his tropical fish and look for his hearing aid. She says he's miserable without it. Can't hear the TV or anyone. It makes it so he shouts, since he can't hear the sound of his own voice."

She glanced sideways at her daughter. "That explains a few things, doesn't it?"

Of course! In an instant everything clicked into place. No wonder Mr. Straub had hollered at Nan. He couldn't hear how loudly he was speaking if he wasn't wearing his hearing aid. The mystery of Jamie's ball disappearing remained. But there was no way to prove Mr. Straub was the person who had found it in the petunia bed. Perhaps some inquisitive child had spotted it and taken it.

When she got home, she tried calling the other kids—first Meg, then Ruth Ellen. Too late she remembered their families were meeting for a quick supper at the pizza parlor. Glenn was Ruth Ellen's brother, so he was with them. She didn't know Skip's phone number.

They were all going to meet at the side of the large white house, in the driveway, at eight. In a flash Julie knew exactly what she would do. Nan and Jamie were in their costumes already and were far too excited to do anything but nibble at the dinner Mom had fixed. Julie ate a few bites and then asked to be excused. Upstairs she found the witch costume and put it on.

"Be sure you have the little ones in bed by eight-thirty," Mom instructed Julie. "That's late enough for them. I'll be home as soon as I can, but I thought I'd keep Mr. Straub company for a while. He has no close relatives."

There was time enough to go up one side of the block and down the other for treats. Troops of small children were making the rounds disguised as pirates and goblins and witches.

Soon Julie said, "Listen, Nan and Jamie. I know something that'll be lots of fun."

Small as they were, the two of them caught on right away to her scheme. They scurried after her up Mr. Straub's drive and hid behind the rhododendron bush.

"You're stepping on me," squealed Nan.

"Shhhhhhh!" whispered Julie. She moved over as best she could. "Scrunch down, you two. Here they come. Jamie, better stop popping that bubble gum. They're sure to hear you."

Four figures tiptoed up the drive. From behind the bush, Julie heard Glenn say, "This is it, gang. Ready?"

"We said we'd give him a chance to answer the doorbell," Meg reminded him.

"But of course we know he won't do it," put in Skip.

"We've got to wait for Julie," whispered Ruth Ellen.

"NOW," whispered Julie to the two at her side. "One . . . two . . . three!"

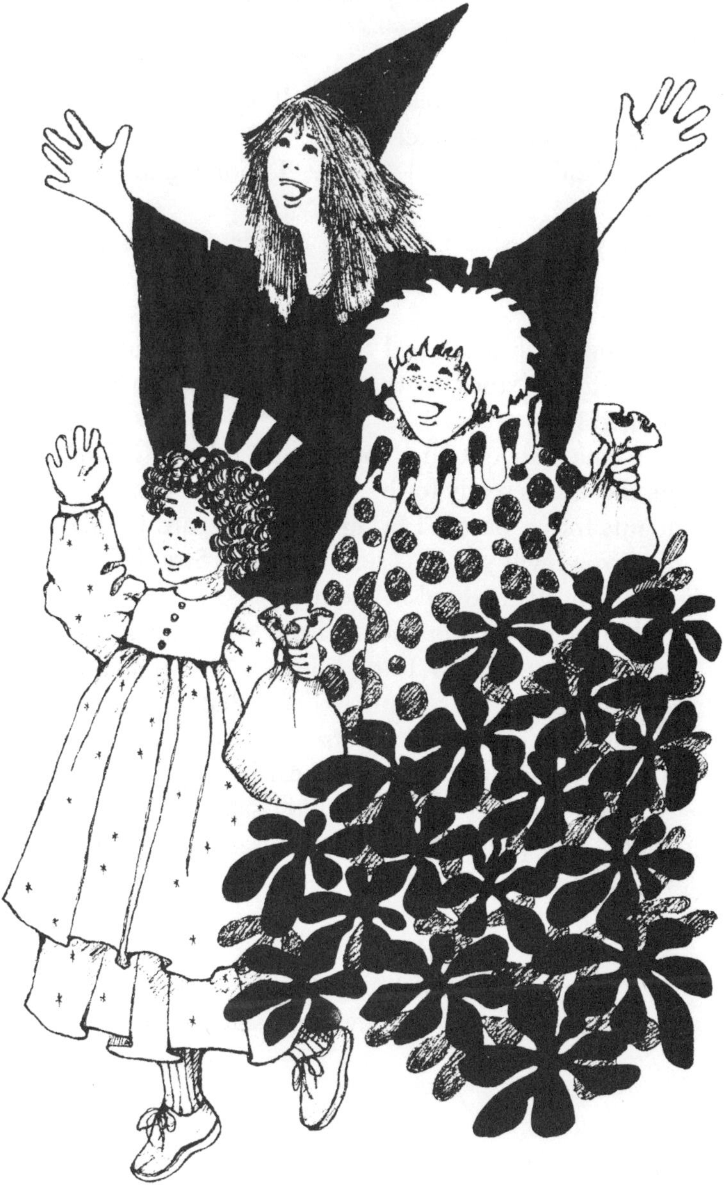

Out into the driveway they tumbled yelling, "*Surprise! Surprise!*"

"I've never been so scared in all my life," confessed Meg a few minutes later.

"Me either," agreed Glenn. "I didn't know what was up."

They were sitting in a line on Mr. Straub's steps, sharing candy from Jamie and Nan's bags as they talked.

"Some trick!" laughed Skip. He blew a bubble so large that it stuck to the end of his nose when he popped it.

"Come on over to my house," said Julie. "I've got to get these kids ready for bed. Mom left some cider and donuts for us. Say, if I bring a get-well card to school tomorrow, will you kids sign it for Mr. Straub?"

Four heads nodded in the dark.

"I'm glad you stopped us from going ahead with the trick," remarked Ruth Ellen. "I just thought of something. If Mr. Straub is deaf, that may be the reason he doesn't get treats ready on Halloween. What is the use when he can't hear his doorbell ring?"

"That's the way I figure it too," said Julie in a low voice. "He's probably not as mean as we thought he was after all."

> For God did not give us a spirit of timidity but a spirit of power and love and self-control.
> 2 Timothy 1:7

I come to you asking for courage, dear heavenly Father, so that I may choose the right way even when my friends beg me to do something I know is wrong. Thank you. Amen

This Present Can't Be Wrapped

I helped to sort out Christmas gifts to fill the bags for people living in the nursing home. Some things were very nice, but lots of the presents were things that residents couldn't use. Why don't people find out what would be good to send each year? And what could I give that the residents would enjoy more than old jewelry and books they can't read?

Colleen and her friends Dee and Jill each picked up a carton of small packages and followed Mrs. Byars into the self-service elevator of the nursing home. They were on their way up to Mrs. Byars' office where dozens of other packages were stacked, ready to be sorted.

"This is a great help, girls," said Mrs. Byars briskly. "If it wasn't for volunteers like you, I don't know how we'd get through the holidays. One hundred and twenty residents . . . that means 120 large red Christmas bags to fill with gifts!"

Miss Martha waved to them when they stepped off the elevator. Her wheelchair had been pulled over to the windows of the recreation room so that she could watch what was going on in the yards of the houses across the street. Colleen had gotten to know Miss Martha a little bit on a couple of other visits.

She knew Lorraine Lively in Room 201, too, and blind old Mr. McAllister down the hall. "Mac" was what most of the nursing staff called him. But there were many people here that she had never met. Today she heard a quavery, high voice that she did not recognize.

"Liza Jane!" the voice called. "Is that you?"

"Who is Liza Jane?" asked Dee. They had taken the packages out of the cartons and were sitting cross-legged on the green and brown carpet of the office, ready to sort them.

"She's Mrs. Rutherford's little girl. At least she *was* Mrs. Rutherford's little girl years ago," explained Mrs. Byars. "She'd be about 75 now if she were alive. According to our records, Mrs. Rutherford is 96. Girls," she went on as she rummaged in her drawer for a pair of scissors. "It isn't possible for churches and others who send gifts to know exactly who needs what item. So read the labels on the outside of each package. I'll help you decide what bags to put the gifts in."

For the first time, Colleen noticed that the rows of empty shopping bags, bright red ones, had the names of the residents clearly printed on the sides.

Jill read the label on a gift. "This one says 'Kleenex,

man or woman' and this little flat package says 'Slippers, medium.'"

Dee frowned. "Kleenex for a Christmas gift?"

"It doesn't sound very interesting," chimed in Jill.

"Well, here are three packages labeled jewelry," said Colleen.

"Put the Kleenex in Mr. Mobley's bag," directed Mrs. Byars. "And the slippers in the bag for Miss Martha. She scuffs her feet along as she rolls her wheelchair. She uses up several pair of those knitted slippers each year."

"May I take a peek at the jewelry?" asked Colleen.

"Might as well. If it's earrings, I know somebody who'll enjoy them."

Quickly Colleen pried the tape off one end of a small package. "These are *broken* earrings," she said in a shocked voice. "Old junky ones. Who would wrap up old broken earrings as a Christmas gift?"

"Someone who doesn't know any better," said Mrs. Byars. She was busy reading labels and tossing packages into the different bags. "Throw those in my trash basket, Colleen. It doesn't happen very often. Most of the things are very nice."

"Here's a beautiful bed jacket." Dee held it up for everyone to see.

Mrs. Byars smiled. "There now, that's better, isn't it? Mrs. Dickens will love that. Her circulation is poor. Jill, I see you have a disposable razor. Only one or two of the men are able to use those. Set it on the end of my desk and I'll think of someone."

The four of them went on sorting for the next hour. There was not enough time to inspect every package, so Mrs. Byars suggested that they open only the pack-

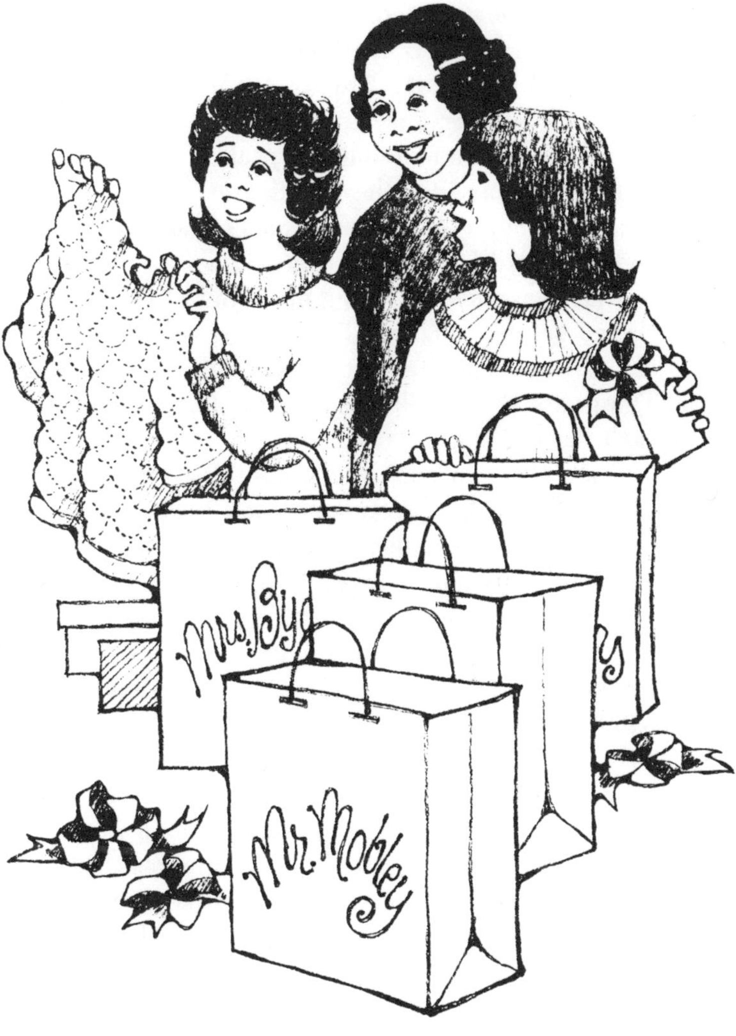
Mr. Mobley

ages that looked suspicious, or the ones without labels.

Jill came up with a pair of slippers that looked as if they would fit a six-year-old child. "Why do people do that?" she wondered crossly. "How would *you* like to unwrap a pair of slippers you couldn't wear?"

"Most of these gifts, like Mrs. Byars said, are OK," said Colleen. Her cheeks were pink from trying to rush through the mountain of packages on the floor in front of her. "But the things are so *dull!* I think Miss Martha has about three cans of talcum powder and a box of Kleenex in her bag."

Mrs. Byars held up a bag made out of bright, crocheted granny squares. "This has a good strong handle. She can hang it on her wheelchair. She'll love it. Things are always falling out of her lap and then she can't reach them."

Gratefully, Colleen reached for the bag and rewrapped it with a pretty green and gold bow.

"What about the people who don't know what is happening anymore?" asked Dee.

"We fill bags for them too," Mrs. Byars told her. They need slippers and bed jackets and other items, you know. And sometimes the most unexpected thing will bring a response. One old man who hadn't said a word since the day his daughter checked him in actually smiled and said "Pretty" when a volunteer left a jar of daisies on his stand last summer."

Someone was calling her on the intercom. Before she left the office she said, "You girls go right on working. When I get back we'll take a break and have some cocoa and cookies."

"It will go more quickly if one of us stands over by

the bags and the other two peek in the packages and toss them," decided Colleen. She didn't know about Jill or Dee, but her head was whirling. She was trying to think of something she could put into every single bag that would seem like a special gift. A paper flower maybe. She knew how to make those from pipe cleaners and colored tissue paper.

Christmas was just two weeks away. She still had Daddy's birdhouse to finish. Would there be time, with help, to make 120 paper flowers? She didn't think so.

The system of tossing packages to Jill and letting her fill the bags worked, although once or twice Colleen couldn't help wishing there was time to open every single one of them to make sure there were no more broken items.

She tried whispering what Grandma called "on-the-spot prayers" under her breath: "God, I keep asking you about little things that don't matter to the rest of the world. But this time it's important. Please make it so the things in these packages are clean and neat."

"Why, how busy you've been!" exclaimed Mrs. Byars when she returned. "You're done!"

When Colleen told her about the idea of putting something special into each bag, she said, "You're right, it is late to start that type of project this year. But I know something every single resident in this nursing home would appreciate more than a package they can open on Christmas Day. A visit. Some of these people have relatives who come regularly, but many have no visitors at all. It is very sad, but true."

"We can do that!" exclaimed Jill. "We'll start dur-

67

ing Christmas vacation. You give us a list of names, Mrs. Byars. The nursing home smelled icky to me when I first came, but now I'm getting used to it."

Mrs. Byars smiled. "That's the disinfectant," she said.

"I've thought of something else," said Colleen thoughtfully. "If you tell me who is having a birthday each month, I'll make birthday cards for them."

The idea of opening a prettily wrapped gift and finding nothing but a box of Kleenex had made her feel very sad, almost as if she wanted to cry. But birthday cards . . . it was a cheering thought. Already she was thinking of a special card for Mr. McAllister, the blind man—a card that he could *feel*.

> He who oppresses a poor man insults his Maker, but he who is kind to the needy honors him.
> Proverbs 14:31

Lord, too often I forget people who have special problems and needs. Help me pay attention to the aged, the sick, the people who are lonely. Show me ways to bring your love to them. Amen

Candy Finds a Way

How can I write a thank-you letter for a gift I don't like? Would it be dishonest to pretend? The person who sent the gift lives far away and would never find out.

"I've finished every note except Aunt Edna's," announced Candy. "Hey, Peter, pass the popcorn. The rest of us want some too, you know."

She grabbed a handful of the buttery kernels and stuffed them into her mouth before handing the big wooden bowl to her mother.

"Could I leave that one note until tomorrow, please?"

Several years ago the Plummer family had started the custom of staying home the first Sunday afternoon after Christmas to write thank-you letters. Daddy always built a roaring fire in the fireplace and

69

Mother saved one canister of Christmas cookies for the occasion. This year Peter had added two batches of popcorn, not because it was needed but because he enjoyed shaking the popper and watching the kernels explode into balls of white fluff.

It was growing dark outside. Candy got up from the folding table they'd pulled close to the fire and knelt to plug in the colored tree lights. Before sitting down again, she flipped the carol record over to the side that had her favorite, *O Little Town of Bethlehem.*

"Leave the drapes open," suggested Mother, "so people passing by can see our Christmas tree."

Eyes pleading, Candy turned to face her. "Please, Mom," she repeated. "Can I do Aunt Edna's letter tomorrow?"

"No fair!" exploded Peter. "If she gets to skip one, I do too."

"But Aunt Edna made you something you can use," protested Candy. "She made you mittens, Peter, and you lose so many mittens you could do with a dozen pair every winter."

Sparks flew up the chimney as Dad stirred the fire. The new log began to crackle. Candy caught her parents' eyes meeting in a silent question.

"We began this letter-writing afternoon so that nobody's thank-you note would be forgotten . . . ," began Mother.

"Run get the hat, Candy," suggested Dad. "Perhaps if you look at it again you'll think of something good to say."

Inwardly Candy groaned. That was the one rule they'd made up about the contents of the letters.

Nobody could get off the hook by scribbling "Dear Uncle Jim . . . thank you for the book. We had a good Christmas. Love . . ."

The ugly blue and green and pink and yellow striped hat was buried under her new ice skates and photograph album. She dug it out. Bringing it to the little table, she sat down and twirled it on one finger without saying a word.

Mom's ballpoint pen paused in the middle of a line. She looked up with a smile. "Can't you at least tell her that you like the bright colors?" she asked.

"But I *don't* like them," wailed Candy. "All those blues and greens and pinks look horrible together. And none of the stripes go with my red jacket."

The expression on Dad's face was thoughtful. Candy detected a trace of sadness, too, as he spoke. "Your Aunt Edna—really she's my Aunt Edna and your great aunt—has always crocheted a lot of afghans. Being a thrifty woman, she thinks up ways to use her leftover scraps of yarn. I'm sure that's why there are so many colors in your hat."

He said no more. Candy knew he must be thinking of the good times he'd had as a boy visiting his aunt's home in northern New York State. It was funny how time changed people. The Aunt Edna Daddy often told about was a small, vigorous woman who split her own kindling and baked as many as six apple pies in an afternoon when she expected a crowd for dinner. The Aunt Edna that she knew was a frail old lady with short, flyaway, snowy white hair and fingers twisted with rheumatism.

The rest of the family had finished their letters. Mother got out her address book and some stamps and began to recheck a few of the carefully written blue envelopes Candy handed to her. The letter to Aunt Edna lay unfinished on the table. Mom hesitated, then patted Candy on the shoulder.

"All right; leave that one for a day or so," she agreed. "Why don't you mention the problem to God when you say your prayers tonight?"

Peter hooted at the suggestion, and Candy looked surprised.

Set deep in a rugged face, their father's blue eyes twinkled. "You children never cease to amaze me!" he exclaimed. "Do you think God is only interested in big problems like war, or world hunger, or keeping me safe when I'm working over at the shipyard?" He winked at Mom because she was the one who worried most about his safety.

"God doesn't pay attention to *hats!*" scoffed Peter.

"You think he doesn't?" persisted Dad. "Well, he *does* pay attention to problems, son. That I know. Through the years he's paid plenty of attention to mine, large and small."

He stood up and ran his hand through his dark hair. Then he walked around to where Candy sat crouched over the table looking miserable. She could feel his strong fingers rubbing her shoulders. Somehow that made her feel better than any of the words which had been spoken.

"Take my advice," he whispered in her ear.

Slowly she nodded. "I'll try."

It did seem silly, praying about a dreadful-looking striped hat. But she had promised, so that night after her teeth were brushed, she knelt by her bed in the dark and murmured, "Dear God, I'd like to throw

Aunt Edna's hat into the give-away box. I'm afraid my friends will laugh if I wear it, but help me to find *something* I like about it so I won't hurt Aunt Edna's feelings when I write to her. Amen."

The rest of vacation whizzed by with so many things to do that Candy put the unfinished thank-you note out of her mind. She and her friend Theresa skated almost every day at the ice rink on the mall. When school started again, the blue note lay behind the clock on the mantel, forgotten.

Once, just once, Candy noticed it when she dusted the living room. Each person in the family had a weekly job. It had been that way ever since Mom had started working part-time in a dental office. Some of the jobs seemed more tedious than others, thought Candy to herself as she dusted the tops of the books and the white china lamp. Like scraping dinner dishes. Oops! She hummed a little tune, trying not to think about the folded bit of blue letter paper she'd seen. Her prayer about the hat seemed to have gone unanswered.

In northwest Oregon the winters were raw and cold and rainy. Whenever snow came the flakes were big and wet and hardly stayed on the ground for more than a half a day. But one day early in January when Candy looked out the window of her classroom, she was delighted to see snowflakes falling fast and heavy.

"They're sticking to the car tops and the sidewalk!" she gloated at lunchtime. "Theresa, Rachel, come on home with me after school. Looks as if there'll be enough for a snowball fight."

From three-thirty until long after the street lights flicked on, the children played in the fresh snow. Peter and his friends worked on a snowman in the front yard while Candy and some of the older girls challenged several neighborhood boys to a fight. As soon as the snowman was finished, the younger children joined the fun.

At dinner Peter reported gleefully. "Everyone on the block says they can stay out until eight tonight. As soon as I finish eating, can I go too, Mom? I'll wipe up the table when I come back in."

Candy's eyes sparkled at the thought of the unexpected treat of playing in the snow after dark. But then she saw her mother's troubled eyes.

"Candy, your red jacket is absolutely soaked. You'd catch cold if you went out in it again. And your old blue jacket doesn't have a hood."

"MOTHER!" Candy begged. "Just this once? I'll take a hot bath at eight."

Nothing she could say persuaded her mother to give in. "Hang your wet jacket over the back of a chair and set it by the register where the heat comes up," said Mother. She went right on scraping dishes and running water into the sink as if this was a normal evening.

Candy wanted to stamp her foot and shout. As if that would do some good! She could hear children beginning to gather outside on the snowy lawns. The doorbell rang and she ran to answer it.

"Come on! Hurry up so we'll have lots of time," said Theresa. "The weather report said it's going to snow all night. My father thinks there won't be any school tomorrow. The buses won't be able to make it up and down the hills."

"I can't," Candy started to say. But an idea popped into her head. "Wait, Theresa, I'll be back in a jiffy." She raced to find the striped hat Aunt Edna had made. Where had she shoved it? On her top closet shelf? Ah, here it was, beneath her sweaters in her dresser drawer. Wearing her raggedy old blue jacket and gloves, and the striped hat, she dashed out to play.

The snowflakes fell on and on. With the Christmas hat pulled down over her ears, and her hair tucked way up inside it, Candy felt cozy and happy.

"That's a neat hat!" cried Rachel. She was racing around through the backyard trying to catch Candy with a snowball. The snowball flew wide of its mark and both girls collapsed laughing. "Wish I had one like yours. Mine is so small my hair gets soaked. Besides, it's black. I love bright colors."

"It is a nice hat," answered Candy. "My Aunt Edna made it for me. Come to think of it, she might have enough leftover scraps to make one for you, Rachel." She looked at her friend and grinned. "I'm going inside now to write and tell her this is a good hat for snowstorms. See you tomorrow."

Her prayer had been answered after all! Of course God hadn't sent the snow just so she would change her mind about the hat. But maybe he had made her grow up enough to figure things out for herself.

Dad was right. It was worth bringing the little problems to God in prayer as well as the big ones. And then, thought Candy, you had to be on the alert.

The answer did not always turn out to be the one you expected.

> Are not five sparrows sold for two pennies? And not one of them is forgotten before God. Why, even the hairs of your head are all numbered. Fear not; you are of more value than many sparrows.
>
> Luke 12:6-7

Help me to bring all of my problems to you, Lord, even the ones that don't seem too important. That is a good way to remind myself how much you care for me, a child in your kingdom. Help me to know the way you would have me go and the things you wish me to do. Amen

The Gift of a Week

I get tired of having the rest of my family mess around with my stuff. Sometimes I wish I were an only child. Is that selfish, Lord?

"I get to watch Sammy Snooper cartoons," shouted Donnie.

"No you don't. Mom promised I could watch *Another Planet*," yelled Rob.

Perched on a kitchen stool, Judy sighed. It was the same old Saturday morning squabble. Suppose she marched into the living room and announced to the twins that neither she nor Margo had watched the *Stars Contest Show* for two whole weeks? Knowing she'd probably lose the battle, she spooned the last drops of sugary milk from her cereal bowl, grabbed her library book, and went out to plop in the lounge chair on the patio, away from the noise.

Mother looked up from the row of pansies she'd been setting out along the edge of the brick garden walk. "Want to help?"

Judy shrugged. "Oh—well, maybe." Tossing her book on the picnic table, she rummaged in the apple crate full of tools. Trowel in hand, she knelt on the ground near her mother.

A muffled wail floated through the open kitchen window.

"It's those twins fighting over TV programs again," sputtered Judy. "Sometimes I wish I was an only child. Take today," she went on angrily. "Margo hopped out of bed and took off for Camp Fire wearing my last pair of clean socks, without asking me for them. Then when I began to hunt around for my Monopoly set, I discovered Phil had left it over at the Rankins' house." She scowled. "I was looking forward to getting up a game this afternoon, but the Rankins won't be back until Sunday night, so no game."

"Sometimes life in a family of five children does get complicated," agreed Mother. Deftly, with the kitchen paring knife, she loosened a purple pansy from its little green plastic container and handed it to Judy. "This dark purple will go well with the pale yellow one I just planted, don't you think?" She smiled. "Perhaps now you can guess why I enjoy gardening so much."

"It gives you some quiet time alone," said Judy. She sat back on her heels, holding the pansy carefully in both hands. "Mom, do you mean it's not wrong for me to wish that everyone would go away and leave me by myself sometimes?"

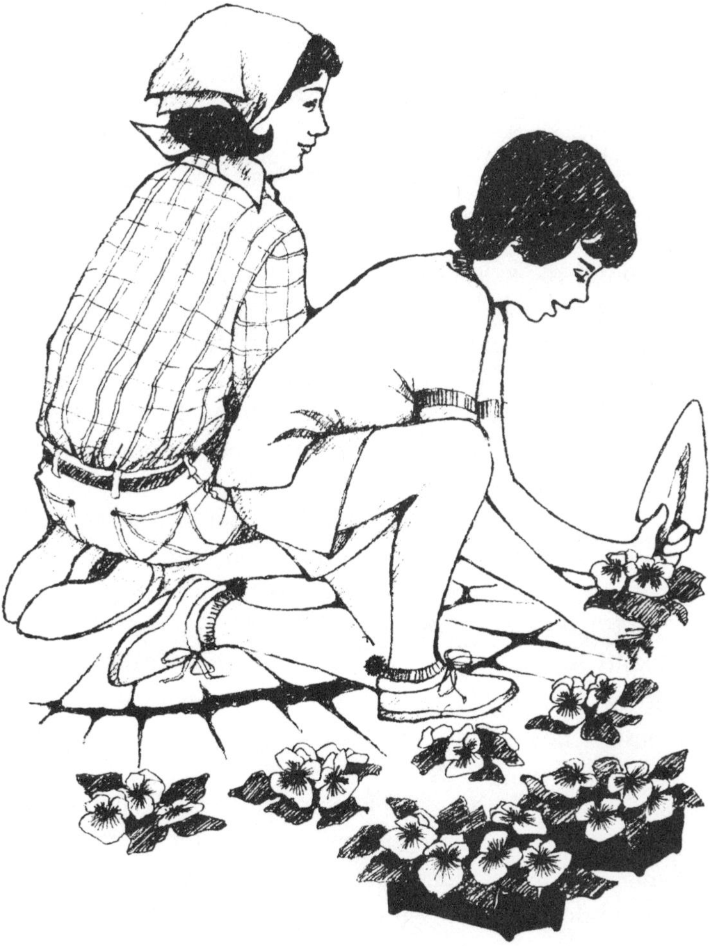

"Indeed no!" exclaimed her mother with a smile. "You're two years younger than Margo, Judy. And the year you started kindergarten, when all my friends were saying to me, 'Oh, don't you hate to see her go?' I used to laugh and tell them, 'Quite the opposite. I've been longing for the day when every child would be in school. I *need* a few hours alone.'" Remembering, she laughed a little before going on. "You know what I did that year? I found a good baby-sitter for the twins and treated myself to two entire mornings a week, all to myself."

"That's what I'd like to do sometimes too," burst out Judy.

"You'll soon have your wish," boomed a voice. Around the side of the house came the end of a ladder followed by her father. Leaning the ladder against the house, he mopped his forehead with a rumpled handkerchief and said, "It's about time I hosed the leaves out of those gutters. Eyes smiling, he glanced at his daughter. "You mean your mother hasn't told you yet?"

Bewildered, Judy stared at both parents. Mom said quickly, "No, Hal. I guess I was afraid the idea would upset her. But now I see it probably won't."

"What idea?" demanded Judy. Surely nothing could be too wrong. Beneath the wide brim of her straw sunhat, Mom's face looked warm and alive. Before answering, she busied herself with another pansy.

"In exactly three weeks the twins will be going off to Bible camp. Your turn will come later in the summer, of course. Since Pastor Lund's wife is one of the counselors, Pastor will need Margo to take care of their two children that week. She'll take the bus over to their house and stay from nine until five each day. He may want her some evenings too. And Phil will be in Idaho at his Scout jamboree."

"So that leaves only me at home with you and Daddy!" cried Judy. Her eyes lit up. She added quickly, "I'm glad Margo will be coming home to sleep. I don't believe I'd enjoy being alone at night, even though we argue a lot. We play games in the dark, you know, and talk."

"Lend a hand with the hose," her father called from the low roof. "Judy, when I holler again, turn the spigot on, please."

"Sure!" said Judy with a big smile. Suddenly she felt much better. But how would she ever manage not to look too happy that the rest of the kids would be away for an entire week? Her reaction was certainly the opposite of the one Mom had expected her to have.

The twins and Phil left on a Sunday afternoon. That evening after dinner when the girls got out the ingredients to bake chocolate chip cookies, Margo giggled and said, "Doesn't it seem strange not to have those boys in here snitching chocolate chips before the cookies are in the oven?"

"To me it feels nice for a change," declared Judy, munching a few of the chocolate bits herself. She stared at the large mixing bowl full of margarine and sugar. "This time we didn't have to triple the recipe though. Dad and Mom and you and I can't possibly eat all these cookies."

"We'll freeze some," said Margo.

The very next morning Judy opened her eyes especially early. She lay there in her twin bed wondering what had awakened her. The bed next to hers had been neatly made and the small clock on the bookcase said only eight-thirty.

"Oooooh," she sighed out loud. "So that's it! Margo's gone already." Barefoot, she pattered into the living room where her mother was reading the newspaper and drinking a cup of coffee.

"You're up early on a summer morning. Did the quiet wake you?" asked Mother. "Margo went off on the eight o'clock bus."

"It feels a little funny being here by myself," Judy told her. "Laura's the same age as the twins, you know, so she's away at the Bible camp too. And Doris is spending a couple of weeks with her cousins."

"You and I have so few chances to do things together," said Mother. "I thought today you might like to walk over to the shopping center with me and look for some material for slacks. You can pick out a pattern for yourself. And we could have lunch at the pizza parlor too."

They ended up doing so many errands, in fact, that they practically had to run home. "I forgot to tell Margo to take her key," puffed Mother, doing her best to keep up with Judy. "She'll be tired and it's too hot for her to be waiting there on our steps."

The next morning Judy said, "Mom, do you suppose you could show me how to make those slacks?"

Together they pinned the pattern pieces on the green material she had helped to pick out. When everything was cut, Mother showed her how to match notches and get the right pieces of fabric together.

"Look!" Judy cried as soon as Margo walked in

late in the afternoon. "See what I've been doing today?" She was glad to see her sister. Mom had stopped sewing at four to meet Dad at the park for a set of tennis.

"You want to put on our suits and have a swim before dinner?" asked Judy. But Margo shook her head.

"Sorry. By the end of the week I'll be getting used to this job. But right now I'm ready to drop."

Judy followed her sister into the bedroom and sprawled on the bed to chat with her while she changed to a different pair of shorts. "These are still damp from the hose fight I had with Ruthie and George," said Margo smiling. Draping herself across the other bed, she nibbled the candy bar Judy offered.

"You'll have some energy after dinner," said Judy. "And there'll still be time for a swim. . . ." Her voice trailed into silence. Margo was sound asleep!

She tiptoed out to the patio and, a little disconsolately, watered the pansies she and Mother had planted.

"Let her sleep," murmured Mother when she came home. She set her tennis racquet in the corner of the breakfast nook and went on, "We should be getting a note from the twins soon. I wonder how they're making out."

"Probably giving their cabin counselor a terrible time," said Dad. At the table, when dinner was ready, he looked over at Judy. "Will you please pray tonight, Judy?"

Tuesday night was usually Phil's turn to pray. But he was far away in a tent some place, where not even a letter could reach him.

"Thank you for this food," said Judy softly, her head bowed. "And please, dear Lord, take care of . . . of members of our family who are away this week."

Eyes still closed, she could feel her father's strong fingers closing over her own as he reached out to hold her hand. He must have heard the quiver in her voice.

"A little lonesome?" was all he said.

During the next two days she wandered about the house, peeking first into David and Rob's room which looked far too neat this week, and then into Phil's tiny, cluttered bedroom at the back of the house. Through the years her older brother had collected curious artifacts from many different places. Knowing he wouldn't mind if she looked at them, Judy sat down in his desk chair for a few minutes.

Here was the piece of petrified wood he'd found one summer; and here was the sheep skull. And the rattles from a snake his Scoutmaster had killed on a camping trip. Gingerly she touched the rattles, smiling to herself as she recalled how frightened she had once been of them. "Ugh!"

She buried her head on her arms. "Oh, Phil! Phil! I never did tell you it was OK about the Monopoly set. And now—suppose something happens and you don't come back?"

Accidents did happen. Suppose Phil chopped his foot with an ax, or his tent got caught in some sort of a flash flood? Terrible thoughts continued to spin inside her head until finally she pounded the desk and said, "God, don't you let those bad things happen. I know you won't!"

That made her snicker. Who was she to give God commands, anyway?

The postcards which arrived in the mail on Friday made her more lonesome than ever.

"I'm bringing a frog named Archibald when I come home," wrote David in a scrawl that was hard to decode.

"Tell Judy and Margo hello," scribbled Rob. "I miss them."

"I sure miss them too!" exclaimed Judy. "Mom, I'm so mixed up. First I wanted to be alone here with you and Dad. And then, when I was given the chance . . . ." Her cheeks grew rosy as she tried to think of a way to explain what she meant.

Her mother sat down on the couch beside her. "Remember what I told you about the year you started kindergarten? I could hardly wait for you to get out the door. But Judy, let me tell you the rest of the story. After three hours by myself, I looked forward to having the front door fly open and hearing you shout, "It's me! I'm home!" She put her arm around her daughter's shoulders and gave her a squeeze. "Know that feeling?"

Judy nodded. "I can hardly wait to see Dave and Rob and Phil. Margo's job will be over and everyone will be around again. I'm *glad* I'm really not an only child. It's too QUIET."

Mother chuckled. "Your father will get a laugh over that," she commented dryly. "Perhaps God gave you this week as a gift, Judy, so you'd truly come to value your brothers and your sister."

Judy's eyes were very bright as she answered, "I've thought of a way to show him I got the message. Could we have a homecoming party Saturday night when we're together again? I'll help make the spaghetti. And," she smiled, remembering how many cookies had been left over after she and Margo had baked, "there's plenty of dessert in the freezer."

> Behold, how good and pleasant it is when brothers dwell in unity!
>
> Psalm 133:1

Dear Lord, thank you for letting me see how much each member of my family means to me. Show me how to help things run more smoothly in our home. Amen

Hurrah for Grandma!

There are days like today when I don't want to speak to God. If he's supposed to be such a good, loving heavenly Father, why does he let such cruel things happen in his world?

"Joanne, go save that corner table for us," directed Barbie. "Wait 'til you hear what happened to Heidi's grandmother. Everyone's talking about it."

Nudging her way through the chattering crowd of boys and girls, Joanne reached the far end of the school cafeteria. She had set the alarm early this morning in order to pack tuna fish and pickle sandwiches for herself. Lunch period was short enough without having to spend 10 minutes of it standing in line to buy food.

"Barbie . . . Heidi . . . Sue . . . over here!" she

mouthed the words, waving wildly so her friends would be sure to see her.

"It's awful," said Barbie indignantly as she set down a tray containing a red Jello salad and two mustard-smeared hot dogs in toasted buns. She opened her carton of chocolate milk, stuck a straw in the top, and took a long slurp before going on. "Here's Sue and Heidi now."

"What happened, Heidi?" demanded Joanne. "Everybody knows about your grandma except me. Was she in an accident?"

Heidi, a dark-haired girl much smaller than the rest of her classmates, looked different today. Paler maybe; or was it because her familiar merry smile was missing?

"Grandma Wessing walked down to the T and R Market last night to get a loaf of bread. On the way home, when she turned the corner onto her own block, her purse was snatched," explained Heidi.

"Tell her the rest of it," chimed in Sue. "Tell Joanne about her black eye and broken arm. Why don't you say it, Heidi? She was mugged."

"The only reason she got hurt was because she tried to hang on to that navy blue bag of hers," declared Heidi. "It's her favorite, and Grandma's real stubborn. Anyway, she was knocked down and the break was a bad one. Her arm is going to be in traction for at least three weeks."

Joanne saw the tears in her friend's eyes and said quickly, "What a rotten shame! I don't see how anyone could be that mean, do you?"

"Did he punch her in the eye?" Sue wanted to know.

"No. The doctor thinks she must have banged her cheekbone on the sidewalk pretty hard. She lost her social security check and 10 dollars, and her front door keys. My Mom's over at her house today because the lock on Grandma's door is being changed." Heidi bit halfheartedly into the end of a hot dog bun. "You're right, Joanne, some people are so nasty . . . it's hard to believe!"

"It's a wonder she didn't give him a kick in the shins," remarked Barbie. Although every one of them felt bad, her remark made them giggle. It was easy to picture Grandma Wessing, a plump little woman with gray hair and rosy cheeks, tackling a would-be thief.

Heidi looked around the table at her friends and said, "I think it would cheer Grandma up if the four of us dropped by to see her after school. The nurse'll let us go in one at a time. They're looking for ways to keep her spirits up."

"I feel like she's my own grandma," said Joanne that afternoon when they were on their way to the hospital. "I've eaten about a thousand of the cookies she's baked, I guess. Maybe two thousand. And she always checks out my report card."

Barbara grinned. "Remember when my mom was on the late shift at the factory and had to sleep most of the day? Grandma Wessing heard my spelling words that year."

Grandma looked worse than any of them had expected. Her hair, instead of being pinned neatly in a bun, today hung in a long braid with a rubber band on the end of it. And the bulky hospital gown she was wearing looked as if it must be at least a size too large. Joanne was sure the traction contraption holding up Grandma's arm must feel mighty uncomfortable.

Grandma lay there in bed, very still, holding an ice pack on her cheekbone with her good hand. Her eyes were closed.

"It's me, Grammie. I've brought some friends along." The nurse said the four girls could be in the room together for just five minutes.

"Don't you let anybody worry, child," whispered Grandma Wessing. I've got a message for anyone who asks about me. Tell 'em I'm the winner."

Heidi looked over at Barbie and Sue and Joanne. Joanne frowned slightly and shrugged. Each of them patted Grandma's hand and bent to kiss her cheek.

"They won't let us stay longer for fear we'll tire you out," explained Heidi softly. "I'll be back tomorrow, Grammie."

"You remember that message, dear," insisted Grandma Wessing. And then, to the girls' astonishment, with her eyes still closed, she smiled.

They beat it down the hall of the hospital as fast as they could and ran out into the sunshine. Joanne took a gulp of fresh air and said, "Phew! That place smells!"

"It got to me too," agreed Heidi, wrinkling her nose. "I'm going to ask Mom as soon as I get home—I think maybe Grandma got a slight concussion when she hit her head. My folks probably didn't say anything because they thought I'd be upset."

"She did sound mixed up," said Sue.

Joanne was silent. The sight of Grandma Wessing with her eyes closed and her arm high in the air had touched her deep in a place no words could reach.

Her mother was in the kitchen flouring chicken pieces for dinner. Joanne set down her books and said, "I know I'm late, but Mom—it's Grandma Wessing. Did you hear what happened to her? We stopped by the hospital."

When her mother nodded, Joanne continued, "Her arm was broken in three different places. And when she talks, Mom, she doesn't make too much sense. I hope they get that purse snatcher!"

She stormed off to her bedroom to try to do a little math homework before dinner. But her anger, boiling up inside of her, made it difficult to concentrate. When her mother called her out again, her cheeks were blazing.

Because there were just three at home now, with George away at school, they usually sat at the small kitchen table for meals. Mother had set it with pretty gold place mats tonight, and there was a bouquet of daffodils for a centerpiece. And candles too.

"Looks like a party," commented Daddy, sliding into place. "What's the occasion? Have I forgotten somebody's birthday?"

Mrs. Gladstone glanced first at Joanne's burning cheeks and then toward her husband. "A thanksgiving," she said quietly. "For Grandma Wessing's life, and for the fine care she's receiving at St. Helen's Hospital." Briefly she related the story of Grandma Wessing's experience.

Dad's eyes twinkled but he looked sober as he remarked, "Joanne here doesn't look the least bit thankful. Something wrong, honey?"

"I'll say," muttered Joanne with her head down.

"Why are we *thanking God?* I feel like bawling him out! As a matter of fact, I don't want to talk to him tonight. I'm angry that he lets such cruel things happen."

She got up from the table. "You two eat without me. I'm not hungry anyway." Without looking at her parents, she flew down the hall to her room and flung herself on the bed.

She must have fallen asleep. It seemed like hours had gone by when she finally tiptoed into the kitchen to investigate the refrigerator and see what leftovers she could find. Mom had left some pieces of baked chicken and a large portion of tossed salad on a plate for her.

Goodness, the clock on the wall said 9:20!

Voices coming from the living room told her a visitor was in there talking to Mom and Dad. Who would stop by at this hour?

Pastor Thorenson! Too late, she tried to duck back out of sight. She'd forgotten to run a comb through her hair after that long nap. And she was barefoot.

"Never mind the way you look, Joanne," he called in a teasing voice. "Remember, I have three daughters of my own. I'm used to anything."

"You'll be interested in what Pastor's been telling us," said Mother. "He called at the hospital to see Mrs. Wessing. She wanted to know if Heidi had given anyone her message."

"She seemed mixed up when we were there this afternoon," blurted Joanne. "As though she couldn't think straight. She said something about being the winner."

"She wasn't mixed up," reported Pastor Thorenson.

"That woman lives her faith better than anyone I've run across for many a year. I'll explain what she meant in a minute. But first . . . ." He looked carefully at Joanne. "Your parents tell me you're a bit sore with God. Want to talk about it?"

"Sure," said Joanne. "Pastor, if the Lord loves us, why does he let such bad things happen? War, and murder, and mugging?"

"I don't pretend to have all the answers," Pastor Thorenson said thoughtfully. Uncrossing his long legs, he rose from the easy chair and went over to the window where he stood looking out at the darkened street. Joanne knew he must be trying to sort out his thoughts.

When he came back and sat down again, he said, "Let's put it this way. God gave us the will to choose for ourselves how we want to behave, right? You've heard me use the phrase 'free will' in a sermon or two, I believe." He coughed and added with a smile, "That is, if you've been listening to any of the things I say."

Joanne nodded. "You mean Grandma chooses one way to live her life, and the purse snatcher chooses a different way. And God lets them both be free to do that, even when it means somebody gets hurt."

"Great Scott!" exclaimed her father. "I must say I admire you, Joanne, for being able to put it so clearly. That's a very grown-up idea, you know. I've been wrestling with it all of my life."

"Grandma Wessing has a solid faith that sees her through the most difficult circumstances," remarked Mom. "I've known her for many years. I still remember the year she lost a son in the war in Vietnam.

Shortly after that her husband died. I went over to have a cup of tea with her, thinking I might find a way to comfort her."

"And what happened?" asked Joanne eagerly.

Her mother laughed. "She comforted me instead. She shared her favorite Bible verse and told me not to worry; this verse would give her the strength she needed."

"I know the verse," said Pastor Thorenson. "She quoted it to me tonight. It's the one from the 16th chapter of John: 'I have said this to you, that in me you may have peace. In the world you have tribulation; but be of good cheer, I have overcome the world.' You see, Joanne, the thief may have gotten Grandma Wessing's purse, but Grandma was thinking clearly when she told you girls that she was the winner."

Joanne took a deep breath and smiled. "With that kind of trust in God, who could lose?" she exclaimed. "Know something? I don't feel angry anymore."

> He takes no pleasure in causing us grief or pain.
> Lamentations 3:33 TEV

Dear God, when the ways of the world seem difficult to understand, and in times when I feel pain or sorrow, give me the faith to trust that I am a citizen of your kingdom where there is the peace that passes understanding. Amen

There's Room for Three of Us

Nobody in our class wants to sit near the new girl. To tell the truth, sometimes she smells as if she doesn't take a bath very often. I feel sorry for her but she bothers me too. How can I get over it and make friends with her?

Debbie usually scooted right out of her last class for the day, home ec, grabbed her books from her hall locker, and raced for the school bus. She liked to be one of the first on in order to save a window seat at the rear of the bus for herself and her best friend Pam.

The two girls never minded the long ride out into the country as long as they managed to sit together and chat, and maybe get a little social studies homework done too.

Today, though, she'd forgotten the burnt orange

and white skirt she was making. Miss LaMear had asked her to finish the wide ruffle at home over the weekend. Impatiently she pushed her way back up the side staircase against the tide of moving students and down the hall toward Room 106.

Miss LaMear was still there, showing Maria, a new girl, how to measure herself for a pattern. She smiled at Debbie and said, "I do hope Maria here hasn't missed the bus. She lives farther out than you do, Debbie. Hurry, girls. I think you'll make it."

Yes, they'd make it all right, thought Debbie as they tore down the steps. But, being the last ones on, they'd have to sit together in the only seat available, up front behind the driver, Joe Copper. She tried not to look disgusted.

Maria had been at Grable Middle School only a week and nobody wanted to sit near her. For one thing, she was a sobersides, so quiet that she wasn't much fun. Since she spoke Spanish at home, she was hard to understand when she attempted to say things in English. Worse than that, most of the time she smelled. It was only noticeable when you got close to her, an odor of onions and tomato mixed with an indescribable stale smell. The food smells might have been OK, but that sour, unwashed smell was something else.

Debbie scrunched down and let Maria slide in by the partially opened window. With the late spring breeze blowing in as the bus jolted along, perhaps the odor wouldn't be as bothersome. The bus let out an enormous belch when it jerked into motion. She sat down suddenly, clutching her books.

Pamela was probably smirking in the back of the bus. Debbie felt a stab of guilt. Her feelings now seemed to be fighting against everything she'd ever heard in the junior class discussions in Sunday school, and from her mother and father at home. Christians were supposed to be kind to people, but all she could think of at this moment was how long the school bus ride was going to be today because she'd been forced to share a seat with Maria.

As soon as a few kids got off, she supposed she could make some excuse about having to get help with her homework and then move to the back of the bus. But that certainly wouldn't solve the problem of making friends.

"You live out on the Turners' farm?" she heard herself ask Maria. "My brothers and I picked raspberries there last June. It's a pretty place."

She was surprised when Maria shook her head. "Pretty for you, but not for the people who have to live in those cabins," she said in a low voice that Debbie could hardly hear. She turned away and looked out the window of the bus.

After weaving through midafternoon traffic, the bus turned onto the freeway. Four stops and 35 minutes later they would be on the "old road" winding over Wilson Pass and down into the valley where Debbie's family ran the Marston Country Kennels.

Lost in the hubbub of voices around her, Debbie was very quiet. She'd noticed the row of small cabins at the edge of the Turner place last summer, but she hadn't thought much about them. A baby with his diaper falling off had been playing in a mud puddle with his sister, and three men in frayed shirts had been lolling cn the grass drinking beer. That much she remembered. But the cabins?

"They don't look too bad," she ventured to the dark head beside her. Maria had continued to stare out the window as the bus lumbered down the freeway. "The Turners paint them every year, don't they?"

Maria nodded. "But the families who follow the crops from California and other places—they mess them up." She shrugged. "When you sleep six in a one-room cabin, and share a public bathroom with 18 other people . . . ." Her eyes clouded. "There's never enough hot water."

A picture flew into Debbie's mind. She was seeing the gleaming green tile shower in her own home, and the pale pink tub in the larger bathroom at the east end of the house. It was hard work to run a clean, good kennel with only a small crew hired. Her mother and father did most of the work themselves. They expected every one of their four children to help, including six-year-old Damon who had been filling the dogs' water bowls twice a day for almost an entire year. She, Debbie, was responsible for cleaning three of the smaller runs. What would she do if there were no hot shower to pop into every time she came in covered with kennel smells?

"My father is looking for steady work," announced Maria presently.

The crowd on the bus had thinned out. But instead of moving back to sit with Pam, Debbie boldly beckoned her friend to move to the front.

"This is Maria, Pam. Her family is living at Tur-

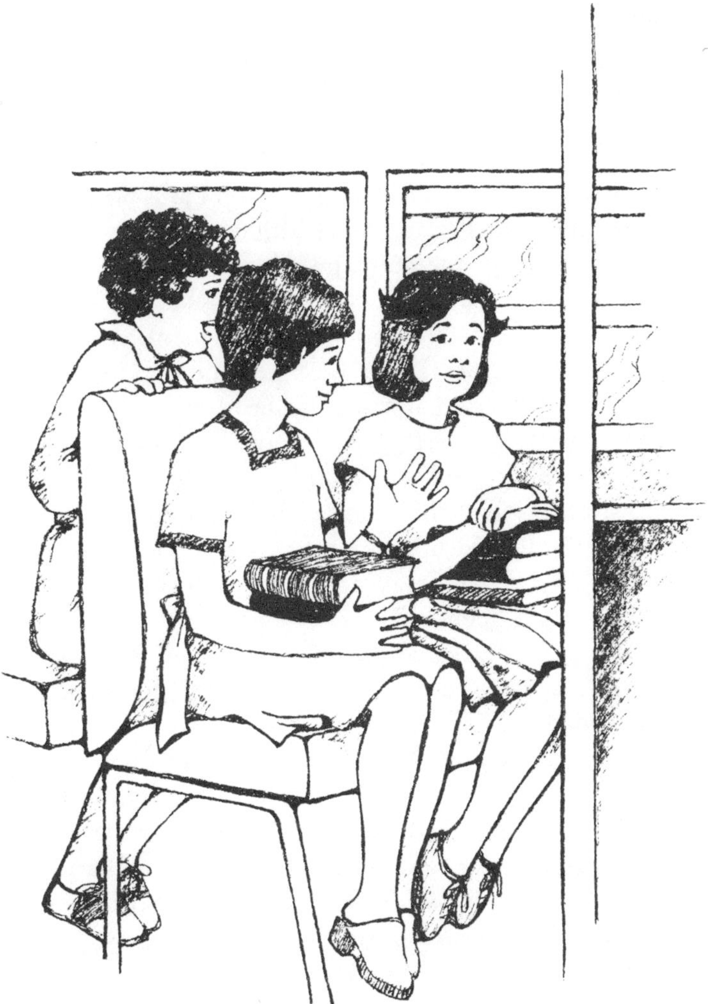

ners' farm." Her warning look would be enough, she hoped, to make Pam keep her mouth shut.

"We've decided, as a family, not to move again," Maria went on in her soft Spanish accent. "My baby sister is sick many days of the year with—what you call it—bronc . . . bronc . . . ."

"Bronchitis," put in Pam, leaning forward to hear better. "Do you know about the free clinic in Carlton?"

Maria nodded. "My father will work. My mother will work. My two older sisters will find jobs also, and finish high school at night. My little brother and I will help take care of the baby, Josephine."

"There are day-care centers," Debbie informed her, bouncing on the seat with excitement. An idea was coming to her but it was the kind of idea that might hurt Maria's feelings if she didn't explain it right. Better wait. Her eyes snapped. "Some of the people at my church sort clothing and pots and pans and stuff to sell at the Migrant League Center."

"My mother spends one afternoon a week there," added Pam. "You may not have heard about it, Maria. It just opened up this spring."

"We heard," replied Maria. "One family tells another. The news travels by the—by the grapevine." She smiled shyly as she used the American expression.

After Pam got off the bus and the two of them were the only passengers left, Debbie tried to choose her words carefully. First she breathed a prayer under her breath: "Dear God, please don't let me embarrass her." Then she spoke in almost a whisper so the bus driver would not overhear what she had to say.

"Maria, I've been thinking. Turners' place is only

half a mile beyond ours. If you get up extra early on school mornings, you know what? You can walk down the road—jog maybe—and grab a quick shower at our house. Then we'll catch the bus together. I'm sure my folks won't mind. We've got two bathrooms. Besides, most of us like to take showers and baths at night after cleaning the dog runs." Her words were coming out in a rush now. "Seems a pity to let all that hot water go to waste every morning."

Maria reached out and squeezed her hand. Her smile was so big and warm that Debbie knew she'd made a new friend. She had one more thing to say before she hopped off the bus.

"That long seat at the very back of the bus is big enough for three of us," she told Maria. "You and Pam and me. And we're the first ones on."

> But be doers of the word, and not hearers only, deceiving yourselves.
>
> James 1:22

Sometimes it is hard to figure out when to say something and when to keep quiet. Give me the right words when I need them, Lord, and help me not to hurt other people's feelings. Amen

The Day of Two Floods

On days when I try hard to do everything right, sometimes things go terribly wrong. These total disaster days leave me with bad feelings. What can I do to get over it?

"I know you'll do a splendid job of taking care of the family, Laura," said Mother right before Daddy drove her to the hospital. "I left lots of spaghetti to warm up; and there's some leftover meat loaf. You know how to make delicious hamburgers too."

She managed a smile, even though she wasn't feeling well, to show Laura what confidence she had in the family. "Get Jimmy to help with Beth. He can keep her out of your hair while you help Daddy get dinner."

"We'll be fine," Laura assured her. "Daddy says we'll be able to talk to you on the phone a couple of days after you have your operation. Did you pack the magazine I bought you, Mom?"

"Right here." Mother patted the pocket of her brown overnight bag. "Bye now."

"Bye!" After the children had waved her off, Laura said briskly: "OK now, I'm boss around here until Daddy gets home." She steadied her voice so the younger children would not know how trembly she felt. Her insides were churning around like they had the day she'd gone out with her Uncle Bart on the charter fishing boat.

The family had known for a week that Mother must have surgery. Dr. Daniels had discovered a small lump that he called a tumor. Only Daddy and Laura and Mother herself knew how serious that could be. If it were cancer she'd be in the hospital for several days. If it weren't, she'd probably be home before next Sunday.

"I'll let you kids know the news as soon as possible," promised Daddy the following morning before he left. "Remember, all those prayers we've been saying are giving your mother lots of strength and courage."

Laura waited and waited for the telephone to ring. Not a single call came in. To help pass the time, she dragged a small table out into the yard and threw a sheet over it to make a tent for Beth and Jimmy. Then she made a big pitcher of lemonade and found some graham crackers. Three-year-old Beth drank two glasses of lemonade, and Jimmy gulped down four before they tackled the plate of crackers. They had been playing hard in the warm July sun.

Laura began to get worried. Not a word from

Daddy! He'd gone off at seven o'clock and it was nearly noon.

A voice behind her made her jump. "I decided to come home and tell you in person."

"Daddy!" she cried. "Quick, tell us, how's Mom doing?"

"The surgery went fine," reported her father. He swooped Beth into his arms and sat down in a lawn chair. "Yes, Jimmy, I'd love a glass of that lemonade."

After a few swallows he said, "Your mother is still sound asleep. I'll go back after a while to be there when she opens her eyes." He grinned. "Laura, Dr. Daniels got every bit of the tumor. It *was* cancerous but he caught it so early that Mother is going to be as fit as a fiddle. They may decide to give her some treatments just to make sure none of those bad cells begin to grow again. The best news is that she'll be coming home Saturday."

The days seemed long without Mother there to help them think of new summer adventures and projects. She was the one who'd thought up the Treasure Hunt game, and when Laura and her friends had made up a neighborhood newspaper, she had typed up the issues for them on her old portable.

Laura decided to write a list of things to do each day—a list of housework jobs like laundry and cooking and a separate list of play activities.

"If we cram every single day full of things to do, Saturday will get here in no time at all," she told Jimmy. "What would you like to do first?"

"Paint the porch," said Jimmy promptly.

"I think that'll have to wait until Daddy's around

to oversee the job," Laura told him. Seeing his disappointed face, she added, "Wait. I have an idea."

She vanished inside the house and came out in a few minutes carrying two sand buckets and a couple of old paintbrushes.

"Watch me, Jimmy. We'll fill these pails with water, and then you and Beth can paint the steps as much as you like, with plain old water. See how it makes the wood look dark? And when it dries you can go over it with a second coat." She grinned. "I bet these steps could use at least *five* coats of water paint this morning."

The next day, after the beds were made and the breakfast dishes washed and put away, the three of them walked over to the wading pool in the park. Some of Jimmy's friends were there already, splashing one another. And Laura's friend Kristen was lying on the grass baby-sitting her little brother.

Kristen had taken her socks and shoes off. "They let kids our age wade in there if we don't get too rough," she said. "C'mon, Laura."

They hooted and hollered and splashed and ran. The park was a wonderful place to play because there were so many things to do—swings and slides, the wading pool, and badminton and a croquet set that could be checked out by the hour.

When they were tired, the girls sat in the cool shade of an elm tree and talked.

"I'll bring Dinkie tomorrow," said Laura. "That poodle just loves to chase butterflies! Besides," she confessed to Kristen, "the more I keep the kids outside, the less clean-up work there is to do."

"Tomorrow the bookmobile will be here," Kristen

reminded her before they parted. "Remember your library card."

"Your mother's pleased to hear how well things are going," Daddy told her one evening. He shot a mischievous glance at Laura as he grated cheese to melt on top of the macaroni dish she had prepared. "She says she may stay in the hospital for an extra day or two of vacation."

On Friday, after dinner, they took their double-decker ice-cream cones out to the porch glider. Laura said, "There are quite a few things I *haven't* done this week. The kitchen floor is sticky; and the bathroom is a mess. And the piano is so dusty that Jimmy was playing tic-tac-toe on the lid this morning."

"We'll get up at eight o'clock," announced Daddy. The place'll be shipshape by the time I pick up your mother."

The next morning, when Laura wakened, rain was drumming steadily on the roof and streaming down the windowpanes. "Nuts!" she muttered. "Now the little guys'll be underfoot. Oh, well. The best way to keep them out of trouble will be to let them help."

They began right after breakfast. "Beth, take this rag and dust the piano," Laura directed. "Climb on the chair to reach the high places. Jimmy, run some water in the tub and scrub it hard. Use plenty of scouring powder."

She hurried to the basement to do the last big load of laundry. While she waited for it to get done, she folded towels from the dryer. When at last she carried the rainbow-colored stack of towels upstairs, the house was extremely quiet.

"Jimmy and Daddy went to get groceries," called

Beth from the top floor of the old house. "Lau-ra! Help me!"

Laura took the steps two at a time. Her bedraggled sister was squatting in the middle of a puddle. Water streamed steadily from sink to floor and out the door of the bathroom.

"Jimmy told me to do the sink," sobbed Beth. Her face crumpled. "Don't spank, Laura! I c-can't turn off the f-faucet."

Laura sloshed into the bathroom and gave the faucet a firm twist. "You were turning it the wrong way, Bethie." She took a deep breath. "Laura's not cross. Go find some dry jeans." Kneeling, she grabbed two of the fluffy blue towels from the stack and resolutely began to soak up the puddle. The sponge mop was in the basement closet, much too far to run in an emergency.

The phone rang. Laura piled the sopping towels in the tub and went to answer it. Uncle Bart, Daddy's youngest brother and her favorite uncle, was on the line.

"How are things going over there?" he wanted to know.

"Not too well," admitted Laura. "Beth flooded the bathroom. Daddy and Jimmy are out getting groceries...."

"That's why I called," said Uncle Bart cheerfully. "They stopped by. They're bringing me home with them. We'll pick up deluxe hamburgers for lunch. All you need to do, my dear, is to put on the water for some tea."

Laura carried the wet towels down to the washer. As she dashed through the kitchen, she turned on

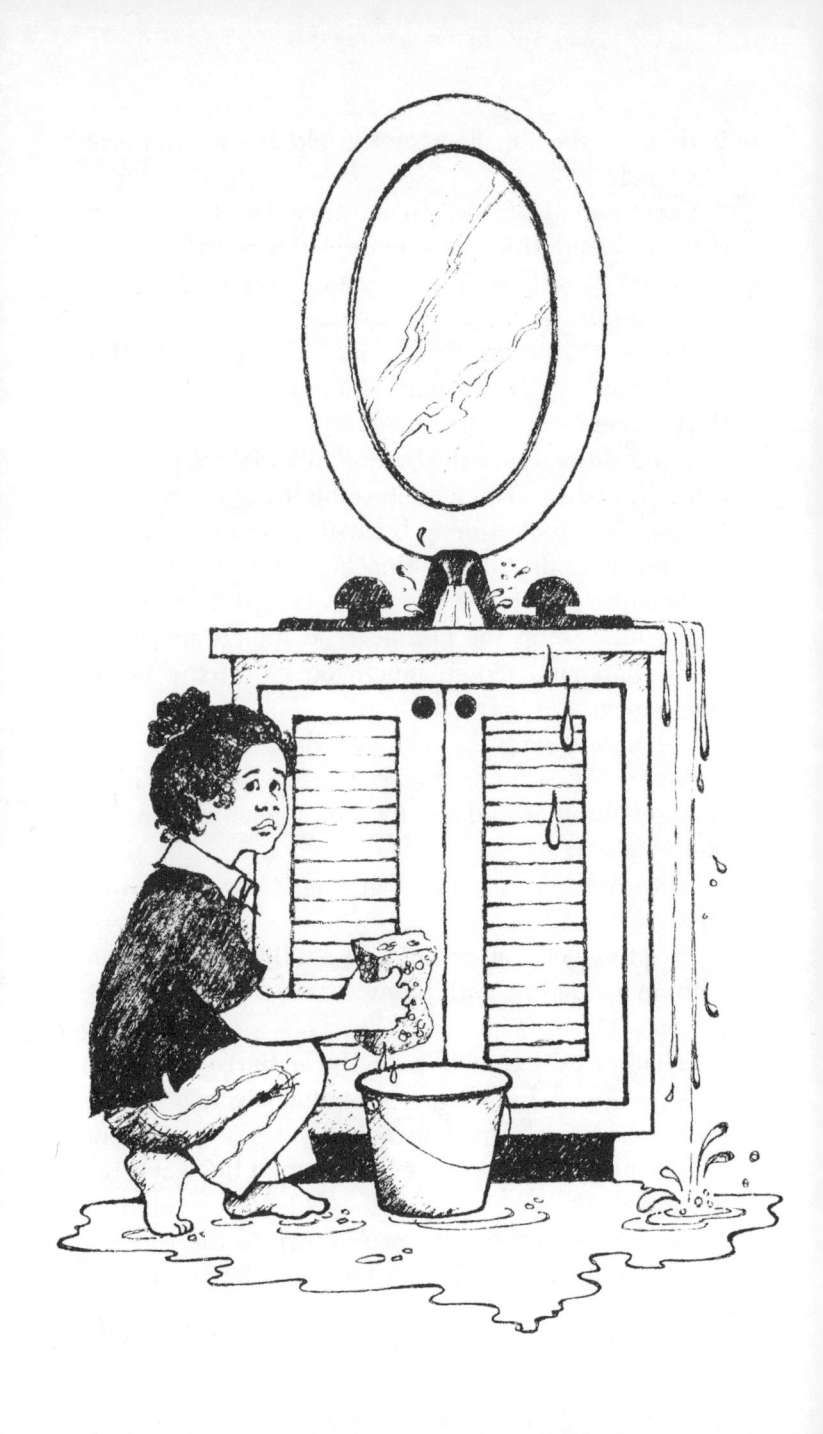

the burner under the teakettle. By the time Uncle Bart and Dad and Jimmy arrived, the washing machine was whirring, Beth was clean and dry and smiling, and the bath mat had been wrung out and hung over the towel rack to dry.

Daddy had worked hard on the kitchen, so they spread the hamburgers and fries on paper plates and ate them at the dining room table.

"Now I know how your mother feels," he told the children, "after she scrubs those counters and the floor and one of us comes along and makes a peanut butter sandwich without putting any of the stuff away."

He was about to say something else but Uncle Bart leapt out of his chair. "Is that smoke I smell? What's burning?"

"It's the teakettle," wailed Laura, racing to the kitchen. "I've burned the bottom out of Mother's new kettle!"

Her father grabbed the asbestos mitt from its hook near the fireplace and hurried in. Gingerly he set the blackened, smoking kettle in the sink. "No use cleaning it. It's leaking. But, Laura, it was an accident. We'll air the place out and I'll scrub the range and sink over again."

After that nothing seemed to go right. Jimmy and his friends tracked mud on the carpet. Dinkie demolished a pile of leftover french fries and got sick behind the lounge chair. Daddy gave his thumb a nasty cut when he was prying bubble gum off the floor with the paring knife. He sucked it, rinsed the blood off, and let Laura stick a bandage on it.

"It's about time for me to go to the hospital," he

said wearily. "We haven't thought about dinner, have we?"

Laura shook her head sadly, then astounded herself by giving way to tears. They came jerking up from some secret place and caught her completely off guard.

"Go ahead and bawl," advised her father gently. He led her to the couch and sat down beside her, motioning the rest of the family to leave them alone. Then, big girl that she was, he drew his daughter into his lap and stroked her hair.

"I wanted everything to look nice for Mother," Laura cried.

"I know," he comforted. "But it isn't your fault that everything seemed to go wrong today. Mother realizes you worked hard all week long. She and I are proud of you." He was quiet for a minute, then added, "There's something else, Laura. You've been feeling bad about Mother's illness. You'll feel much better now that the tears have come out."

At that point Uncle Bart appeared with a box of Kleenex, a pile of paper napkins, and a towel. "A second flood," he exclaimed, without cracking a smile. "I've been assigned to do the mop-up job on this one. Think of it, Laura, what other family on this block has had to cope with two floods in one day?"

Laura gave him a wet smile and said, "Come on, let's get back to work."

"It is beautiful to be home again," said Mother a little later. She'd been smothered with kisses and Jimmy had brought her a bouquet of daisies from the backyard. Beth unlatched her overnight bag and got out her slippers.

Laura was relieved to see that she looked surprisingly well and rested, although slightly pale. When they were alone, she said, "Mom, I burned up your new teakettle."

Her mother's laugh rang out. "Is *that* all?" she asked. "Why, that's only a *thing*, Laura. You didn't break any people, did you? People are so much more valuable than teakettles. And, from what I hear, you've done an excellent job of taking care of people this week." She reached up to touch her daughter lightly on the cheek. "Thank you!"

> For where your treasure is, there will your heart be also.
> Matthew 6:21

Help me to remember to put people before things, Lord, so I can follow your great commandment of love. When the way gets hard, let me draw strength from knowing you are my friend and are always at my side. Amen